OWEN

NO

Plants and Animals

BY LESTINA LARSEN COLBY

Illustrated by James Teason

All About You

BY PAUL NEIMARK

Illustrated by Howard Mueller

MEDICAL CONSULTANT: WERNER CRYNS, M.D.

The Southwestern Company

Nashville, Tennessee

CONTENTS

Plants and Animals

2

All About You

Plants and Animals

Living Things

THERE ARE MANY KINDS of living things. They are of many shapes and sizes. A blue whale is as big as three railroad boxcars. Protozoa are so small that they cannot be seen except through a microscope. Even with a microscope, you can barely see viruses or bacteria. Bacteria are the smallest living things.

Living things are everywhere. They live in water, in the air, on the ground, and inside other living things. They live in very cold places and very hot places. They live in places that are drenched with rain and in places where it may not rain for several years.

No one kind of living thing can live in all the different places on earth. Each kind is especially fitted for living in a particular area. For example, a fish lives very well in water, but it would die on land. A person lives on land but would drown if he tried to live underwater.

Some living things live for only a day. Others live for hundreds and even thousands of years. The oldest known living thing has been alive for 4,600 years. It is a bristlecone pine tree that grows high in the mountains of California. Mayflies, on the other hand, often live just one day.

All living things are able to move. Some like birds, fish, and people can travel from one place to another. A sunflower or a tree stays rooted in one place, but it can bend toward the sun.

Living things can *reproduce*, too. This means that they can produce other living things just like themselves. For example, a cat can only reproduce other cats, and an oak tree can produce more oak trees. Non-living things, like rocks or buildings or chairs, cannot produce new things like themselves.

All living things are made up of very tiny "building blocks" called *cells*. Some living things, like bacteria, are made of only one cell. Others are made of billions of cells. The larger a living thing is, the more cells it has.

Every living thing must have food, water, and air to live. These materials are used to make cells and for the activities of the cell. Living things grow and re-produce by making more cells. In many-celled living things, each cell has a special job to do. For example, some cells of a tree make food, some cells are used to

get water, and some of the other cells let in air. Animals also have special kinds of cells that make up such parts as the heart, skin, muscles, brain, stomach, and eyes.

One-celled living things must also take in food and water and do the other things necessary for life. One tiny cell must do the same kind of things that it takes many cells to do in a large living thing, though it does them in a much simpler way.

Although all living things must do the same things to live, they do not all look or act alike. *Biologists* (people who study living things) divide living things into two large groups—the *plant* kingdom and the *animal* kingdom. Each kingdom includes living things that are very different from those in the other kingdom. In fact, it is usually very easy to tell a plant from an animal. A tree is certainly very different from a dog. Everyone would agree that a tree belongs to the plant kingdom, and that a dog belongs to the animal kingdom.

Nevertheless, there are some living things that cannot easily be placed into one of the kingdoms. In fact, some living things are so simple that they are really neither plants nor animals. Some biologists put these very simple plants and animals into a third kingdom—called Protista.

What Is A Plant?

ANSWERING THE QUESTION, "What is a plant?" is not as easy as it seems. There are many different kinds of plants, and some of them are very different from others.

Many people say, "Plants are green, but animals are not." This is not a sure way to tell whether a living thing is a plant.

It is true that most plants are green, but some plants, like mushrooms and toadstools, are not. And there are green fish, birds, snakes, and insects. These are animals, of course. Color does show one difference between plants and animals, however. All green plants get their color from a material called *chlorophyll*. No animal, no matter what color it is, has chlorophyll.

Green plants can make their own food, using their chlorophyll. Animals cannot make their own food, so they must eat plants and other animals. Plants that are not green cannot make their own food either, because they have no chlorophyll. They must get their food from other living things.

Green plants make their food by *photosynthesis*. This word means "making something with the help of light." Because they need light, green plants can make food only in the daytime. During the process of photosynthesis, the chlorophyll in the plant uses water from the soil and carbon dioxide from the air and makes sugar, the plant's food.

Plants cannot move from one place to another by themselves as most animals can. Only parts of a plant move. Leaves turn toward the sun, and roots grow down to get water.

Plants cannot see, hear, feel, taste, or smell, as most animals can. Plants do not bend toward the sun because they see it. They bend because the sunlight causes the side of the stem away from the sun to grow faster. This curves the stem toward the sun.

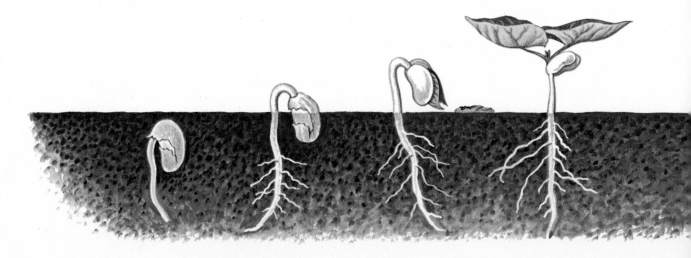

Most green plants grow from *seeds*. Even the biggest tree comes from a tiny seed. The giant redwoods of California grow from seeds less than an inch long.

Seeds are made by the *flowers* of plants. To make seeds, the flowers need pollen. Although most flowers have yellow, dust-like pollen, a flower usually needs pollen from another plant of the same kind to make seeds. Bees and other insects help flowers get pollen. As a bee crawls into a flower to get nectar, pollen gets all over its body. When the bee goes to the next flower, some of this pollen gets on the flower. Wind is also a good pollen-carrier. It blows pollen from one flowering plant to another.

Seeds come in many different shapes, sizes, and colors. They are often red, white, yellow, or brown. Some are so small you can barely see them. Some, like the coconut, are very large. Some, like squash and watermelon seeds, are flat. Some, like pea seeds, are round, and others, like orange seeds, are egg-shaped.

Seeds need to be spread over a wide area so they will have room to grow into new plants. If all the seeds stayed near the parent plant, the young plants would not get enough water or light. Some plants, like dandelions and milkweed, grow seeds with fuzzy parachutes that blow in the wind. Elm and maple seeds have tiny wings and are also blown by the wind. Nuts, as they fall from the trees, bounce and roll to new places. Others, like pansy, violet, and touch-me-not seeds, are shot out when the seed pods burst open.

If a plant grows near a lake, ocean, or river, its seeds float away. Birds carry some seeds as they fly away with fruit to eat. Animals and people carry seeds that stick to their fur or clothing.

In every seed, there is a tiny plant and food for it to use in growing. Peel off the outer coat of a bean seed and carefully split the seed into halves. These halves are the stored food. Between the halves there is a very tiny plant. As the tiny plant in a seed grows, the stem pushes upward through the soil. No matter how the seed is placed, the roots will always grow down and the stem will always grow up.

Soon the new plant has used all the stored food and must start to make its own food. By this time the *leaves* — the food-making part of the plant — are out of the

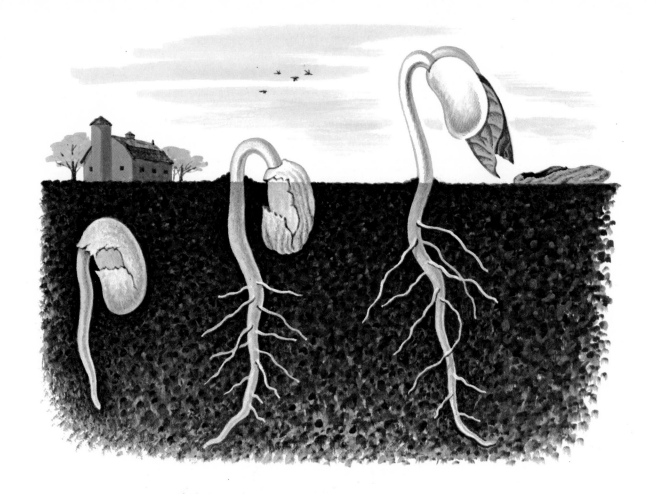

ground. The leaves can get the air and sunshine that they need to make food. The leaves also need water and minerals, which the roots get from the ground. The water and minerals from the roots travel through tiny tubes in the stem up to the leaves.

During the summer when there is plenty of sunlight, the leaves of plants are busy making food. There will be many days during the winter when there are no leaves to make food, and so plants need places to store food. Many of the vegetables we eat are really storage places for plant foods. Some are roots like carrots, beets, and turnips. Onions are special underground storage places called bulbs. Potatoes are underground stems that grow large as they store food.

Trees store food, or *sap,* in their trunks. We make maple syrup from the sap of maple trees.

In the spring the small brown buds that were on the branches of the trees all winter are fed by the stored sugary sap from the trunks of the trees. Slowly each bud opens and becomes a leaf or flower.

The underground parts of plants are very important, too. The *roots* take in water and minerals from the soil. The water and minerals travel up to the leaves, where they are used to help make food for the plants. The roots also help hold the plant in the ground.

There are several different kinds of roots. Each kind is especially suited to take care of a plant's needs.

A taproot is the large main root of a plant. Carrots, beets, and turnips are taproots. They also store food for the plant. Taproots grow way down into the ground to get water. Alfalfa taproots may grow down 15 feet below the surface. It is usually very hard to pull up a plant that has a taproot.

14

Another type of root system has many small spreading roots. These are very shallow and get water from soil close to the top of the ground. Plants like grasses and cactus plants have shallow roots.

Root hairs grow at the tips of the roots. These are very important because they are the part of the roots that take in water. Plants often die if they are pulled up and then replanted because too many root hairs are broken off, and the plant cannot get enough water. When you are replanting a plant, dig carefully around it so that there is a ball of soil around the roots. This will keep the root hairs from being broken off.

The *stems* of plants hold the leaves up to get sunlight. Tubes inside the stems carry water from the roots to the leaves. Other tubes carry food made in the leaves back to the other parts of the plant. Finally, some stems are storage places for extra food that is made by the leaves. The *stem* of a tree, of course, is its *trunk*. A tree trunk does the same important jobs as the stem of a small green plant.

Plant Families

MANY YEARS AGO people thought that there were about 200 different kinds of plants in the world. Today *botanists* (scientists who study plants) have been able to name almost 400,000 kinds of plants. About 2,000 more kinds of plants are being discovered or developed every year.

Each kind of plant has a *scientific name.* Most people do not use these names, though, but call plants by their common names. One plant can have many different common names, which are used in different places. *Pinus ponderosa* is the scientific name for the ponderosa

pine that grows in the west. But in some places it is called the "Arizona pine" and in other places it is called "western yellow pine." There may be many common names for a plant, but only one scientific name.

In order to study the millions of plants, *botanists* have divided the plant kingdom into smaller groups. First, it is divided into two large divisions, or subkingdoms: Thallophyta and Embryophyta.

THALLOPHYTA

The Thallophytes are simple plants, without true roots, stems, leaves, or seeds. Many are one-celled and can be seen only under a microscope. Most of them live in water, in dark, moist places, or even inside other plants or animals. Some are green, like algae and lichens. Others are not green and cannot make their own food. These are the fungi, bacteria, and slime molds.

The *algae* are the simplest green plants. (One plant is an *alga*.) Most algae live in water. Two common kinds are seaweed and the green scum that forms on the top of ponds and in fish tanks.

Fungi are plants that cannot make their own food. (One plant is a *fungus*.) They have to get their food from other plants and animals. Fungi that feed on living things are called *parasites*. If the fungi get their food from dead parts of plants and animals, they are called *saprophytes*. Toadstools, mushrooms, and bracket fungi (which grow on dead logs) are all saprophytes.

Lichens are very odd plants. They are really a fungus and an alga living so closely together that they look like one plant. The alga makes the food for itself and the fungus. The fungus, in turn, stores water and keeps the alga from drying out. Since lichens do not need soil, they can grow in many places—on rocks, on trees, in the desert, and in frozen places.

Bacteria are the smallest living things. They are one-celled, non-green plants. They can live either in dead material or on living plants or animals.

EMBRYOPHYTA

All the plants in the subkingdom Embryophyta re-produce by *spores* or *seeds*. Spores are like seeds except that they are generally smaller than seeds and usually have only a single cell. The tiny plant inside a seed is made of a great many cells.

Mosses and *liverworts* are the only members of one large group of Embryophyta. Millions of years ago these were the first plants that were able to live on dry land. The tiny liverworts are ribbonlike plants that cling very closely to whatever they are growing on.

Mosses usually grow so close together that they form a velvety green carpet. They grow on trees, rocks, and on the ground. They have the beginnings of stems, leaves, and roots.

The other large *phylum,* or group, of Embryophyta contains all the *vascular* plants. These are the plants you probably know best. They have tiny tubes inside their leaves, stems, and roots to carry food and water. Some are seed plants; others do not have seeds.

Ferns, club mosses, and horsetails belong to the non-seed group. They reproduce by *spores.* Millions of years ago giant plants in this group formed huge forests of tree ferns, tree horsetails, and tree club mosses. Now, except for a few large tree ferns in the tropics, all of these plants are very small.

The *seed plants* are the most highly developed plants. They are all green and all grow from seeds. There are *flowering* plants, or angiosperms, and *cone-bearing* plants, or gymnosperms.

Plants like pine, spruce, and fir trees produce *cones.* They never have flowers or fruit. Their seeds grow inside the cones.

There are more kinds of *flowering plants* than all the different types of lower plants put together. The flowers of some plants like the tulip, magnolia, iris, and sunflower, are large and easy to see. Other plant flowers are not so noticeable.

The largest family of flowering plants is the *composite* group. What look like single flowers on these plants are actually a great many tiny flowers, or flowerets. One flower is actually a bouquet. A sunflower, aster, or daisy

The Plant Kingdom

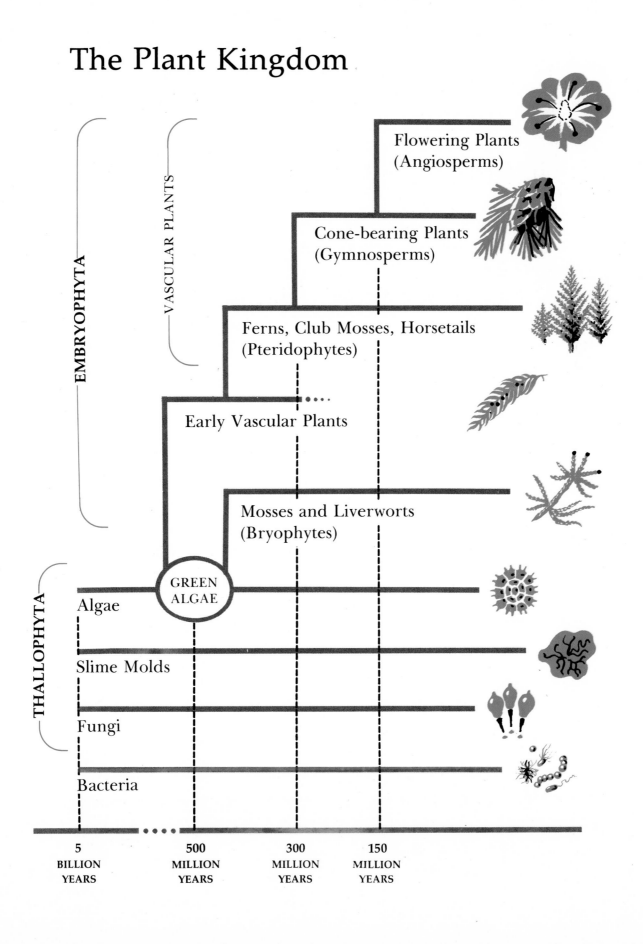

EMBRYOPHYTA

VASCULAR PLANTS

THALLOPHYTA

Flowering Plants
(Angiosperms)

Cone-bearing Plants
(Gymnosperms)

Ferns, Club Mosses, Horsetails
(Pteridophytes)

Early Vascular Plants

Mosses and Liverworts
(Bryophytes)

GREEN ALGAE

Algae

Slime Molds

Fungi

Bacteria

5	500	300	150
BILLION YEARS	MILLION YEARS	MILLION YEARS	MILLION YEARS

may look like just one flower, but there are many flowerets in the center. Other composite plants are dandelions, zinnias, marigolds, lettuce, and ragweeds.

Perhaps the most important family of flowering plants is the *grass* family. It includes not only the grass that grows in your yard, but also the kinds that produce grains or sugar for food. Some of these are corn, wheat, oats, rye, and sugar cane.

The *pea* family is also important. Peas, beans, clover, alfalfa, and peanuts all belong to it. The *rose* family is delicious as well as beautiful! It includes plum, apple, pear, cherry, and peach trees; and strawberries, black-berries, and raspberries, as well as roses. Pumpkins, watermelons, cucumbers, squash, and muskmelons all belong to the *gourd* family.

The *lily* family is full of surprises. Beautiful day lilies, Easter lilies, tiger lilies, tulips, trillium, and dog's tooth lilies are in the same family as onions, garlic, and asparagus.

The *nightshade* family of plants is both useful and dangerous. All its member plants have poisonous parts that can kill people or make them ill. Other parts of these plants are good to eat or are useful in other ways. Nightshade, potato, tomato, tobacco, eggplant, petunia, and bittersweet plants belong to this family.

Ancient Plants

ALL THE LIVING THINGS on earth have changed since life on earth began. Over 500 million years ago, no plants or animals lived on land. The only plants lived in the sea. The plants that first began growing on land were very different from today's plants. Since these early plants have long since died out, the only way we can learn about them is from *fossils*.

One kind of plant fossil is a dent or mark in a rock which shows the shape of a plant. The mark was made in soft clay, which later hardened into stone. It is a picture of what a plant looked like millions of years ago. Other plant fossils are really *petrified* parts of a plant. Minerals, like lime, in the water replaced the original material of the plant, and then hardened. Petrified Forest National Monument in Arizona is a forest of petrified trees.

Probably the earliest plants were much like bacteria. But since they were soft, they could not leave any fossil remains. A few early fossils that have been found were of algae that lived in the water.

Among the first land plants were the Psilopsid. These plants were very much like algae, for they did not have true roots, seeds, or flowers. They were small plants with thin green stems that branched into Y-shaped tops

or ended with cone-like shapes. Tiny hairs held the stems in the soil. It took millions of years for the descendants of these first plants to cover the land with huge forests of giant horsetails, club mosses, and tree ferns.

About 300 million years ago the earth's climate was warm and moist. There were lush jungles of giant ferns. The club mosses were about 100 feet tall, unlike the tiny ones of today. Horsetails grew to be about 40 feet tall, and the tall tree ferns rose 60 or more feet into the air.

These ancient forests were very strange. Some of the "trees" looked like hollow tubes covered with leaves. Some looked like giant carrot tops. Others had leaves that looked like daggers or like tiny fans.

Even though these ancient plants have been dead for millions of years, they are still very important. The fern forests grew in the damp lowlands. As leaves, branches, and trees fell to the ground they were covered with water. Over the years a 40-foot or more layer of this plant matter built up. For some reason a few of these plants became petrified into a material called *coal balls*. The coal balls were very heavy and crushed the other plant debris. Over millions and millions of years of this kind of pressure, the soft plant material was changed into a fairly hard material that burns very easily. It is *coal*. When you use coal in your furnace or fireplace, remember that it is made from plants that lived about 300 million years ago—in a period we now call the Coal Age.

The plants continued to change. About 200 million years ago, the first *conifers* (plants that have cones) started to become more important than the giant ferns, club mosses, and horsetails of the Coal Age. These conifers, the *cycads*, were growing when the dinosaurs roamed the earth. Relatives of this early conifer still live in the warm places of the world.

By the end of the Age of Reptiles, about 70 million years ago, there were flowering plants. Some of the common plants of today were growing. There were oak, maple, elm, and willow trees, and grasses. These plants continued to flourish and soon became the most numerous on earth.

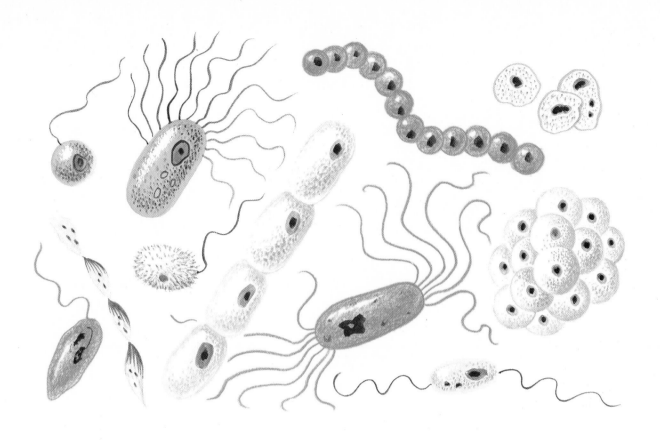

Smallest Plants

A PLANT DOES NOT HAVE to be big to be important. In fact, many very important plants can only be seen with a microscope.

The smallest of all truly living things — bacteria — are found wherever life exists. They live in and on other plants and animals, in dust particles in the air, in the soil, and in the water. There may be as many as 50 million bacteria in a single drop of pond water.

Although bacteria are plants, they cannot make their own food. They must get food from living or dead plants and animals. Many people call bacteria "germs," and think that all bacteria cause diseases. There are about 1500 kinds of bacteria, and most of them are actually harmless. Only a few kinds cause diseases like "strep" throat, pneumonia, food poisoning, tetanus, and tuberculosis. Many kinds of bacteria are actually necessary, useful and important.

Bacteria are necessary for decay. In the woods, billions and billions of these tiny plants are working constantly to cause the decay of plant debris and animal wastes. If these things did not decay, deep layers of dead plants and animals would cover the earth.

Other bacteria help in making cheese, tanning leather, curing tobacco, making butter, and breaking down plant fibers to make rope and linen.

A tiny, one-celled green *alga* called Chlorella may one day be a very important source of food. About a thousand Chlorella plants would fit on the head of a pin. The Chlorella cells have been dried and made into foods such as bread, meat-substitute patties, ice cream, candy, and cookies.

Scientists wonder if this helpful green alga might be a good "lunch" for long space flights. Besides being food for the spacemen, Chlorella makes its own food and releases large amounts of oxygen as a waste product. All it needs to grow is water, light, carbon dioxide, nitrogen, and other minerals. In a space capsule, it would use the carbon dioxide that is breathed out by astronauts, as well as the nitrogen and other minerals from their waste products. Chlorella could use all the wastes of the spacemen and in turn give them the food and oxygen they need during their flight.

Some small fungi are also important. Yeast is a one-celled fungus plant used in making bread. It feeds on sugar. This process is called *fermentation.*

Fermentation helps turn heavy bread dough into light bread. Millions and millions of yeast cells are in one package of yeast. When this is added to sugar and flour in the bread dough, many carbon dioxide gas bubbles form in the dough. These make the dough "rise" and make it light. The alcohol that is also produced evaporates during the baking.

Molds are another type of fungus. These tiny plants can cause great damage to food, clothing, leather, and living plants and animals. Millions of bushels of stored fruit and vegetables are spoiled each year by mold.

On the other hand, some molds are useful. Many kinds of cheese get flavor from the mold that grows inside them. Some very important antibiotic medicines are made by molds. *Penicillin* is made by a blue-green mold like the kind that grows on spoiled oranges.

Biggest Plants

THE LARGEST LIVING THINGS on earth are plants—the giant sequoias and their taller relatives, the coast redwoods of California.

Among these giants, the tallest one is in the Redwood Creek Grove in northern California. This tree rises about 368 feet into the air, taller than a 20-story building. For a redwood, it is quite young, probably not more than 800 years old. Some redwoods are 3500 years old! This young giant will grow even larger.

The giant sequoias are not as tall as the coast redwoods, but they are more chunky. Probably the General

Sherman tree in Sequoia National Park is the biggest. It measures 101 feet around the base and is 272 feet tall. It weighs more than 12 million pounds!

Other kinds of trees grow to be very large, too. The Big Tree of Tule is a cypress tree that grows in Mexico. The bottom of the trunk of this tree is about 160 feet around. It is not as tall as the redwoods, though.

Banyan trees grow in the East Indies. They not only look strange; they also grow in a very peculiar way. Birds drop the banyan seeds into the tops of other trees. The seeds sprout there, and roots grow down to the ground. Branches grow, too, and supports for them grow down to the ground like long canes or crutches. These "crutches" become the banyan's trunks. Eventually the tree on which the seeds were dropped dies.

A single banyan tree may look like a whole forest of trees. Some banyans have as many as 350 large trunks and over 3,000 small ones. The largest known banyan tree covers an area of 1500 feet around its base although it is not more than 100 feet high. It is so big that 7,000 people can stand under it!

Some kinds of *grasses, ferns,* and *seaweed* grow very tall, too. Bamboo is not a tree, but a very tall grass. It has been known to reach a height of 120 feet. Bamboo grows very, very fast. Some kinds can grow 3 feet in one day!

In the very warm, moist areas of the world there are some giant tree ferns, left over from the great fern jungles of long ago. Their trunks are not wood, but they still can grow 60 feet tall.

"The redwoods of the sea" are the giant kelps, a brown algae. They grow from 75 to 300 feet long. These seaweeds are found along the coasts of the Antarctic Ocean and the colder parts of the Pacific Ocean. The plant is a long slender stalk with a large air sac that acts as a float for a circle of long, thin leaves. Off the Cape of Good Hope these kelps form a huge underwater forest 130 miles wide.

Healing Plants

CAN YOU IMAGINE your doctor using a witch doctor's cure if you were sick? It may have happened!

Drug companies and universities have spent millions of dollars on expeditions to learn from witch doctors what plants they use to treat their patients. Many of these remedies are very ancient. In fact, even in the 1800's in America, at least 80 per cent of the medicines came from plants. People dried many kinds of herbs, weeds and other plants in their attics and over their fireplaces and used them to treat illnesses. Doctors also used dried plants to make medicine.

People may have learned about plant medicines by watching animals and then experimenting themselves. Many animals seem to have a natural instinct to eat a certain plant when they are sick. They seem to know which plant will make them well or keep them healthy.

Two witch doctor's poisons used in South America and in Africa to make poisoned arrows are "new" discoveries for modern medicine.

Curare, the South American jungle's deadliest killer, is being used to save lives. This poison kills by making the muscles very limp. The muscles for breathing stop working, too, and the person or animal dies.

Curare remains deadly for as long as 30 years. There is no sure cure for its poison, and even one scratch from a curare arrow can cause quick death.

But in 1938 modern science "discovered" curare's helpfulness. Very small amounts are now used to relax muscles during operations. A doctor does not have to use as much ether or gas to make the patient relax.

Doctors also use curare to help people who have muscle diseases.

The Kombé poison, also used on arrows, is deadly because it slows the heartbeat until breathing stops. But it also contains *cortisone,* which is a drug used to treat the crippling disease called arthritis. Before, cortisone was made only from special small glands of animals. Kombé is an especially important "discovery" because one pound of Kombé seeds gives as much cortisone as 12,500 pounds of beef animals!

For about 2,000 years another deadly plant, the foxglove, was used as a remedy for heart trouble. A medicine called *digitalis* comes from the foxglove plant. It is the drug used most for treating heart conditions. In the late 1700's a doctor learned from an old woman that digitalis would cure dropsy, a heart condition, for it dries up the excess fluid that accumulates in the body of people with dropsy. This remedy has been tested and is still used today. In the last five years digitalis has also been used for two other ailments—glaucoma (an eye disease caused by excess fluid in the eyeball) and muscular dystrophy.

Some plant medicines are very old. Europeans have used *quinine* since 1640 to treat malaria. South American natives used it long before that. Malaria is one of the most serious diseases in the world, especially in tropical countries. Quinine is a very bitter medicine made from the bark of the cinchona tree of South America. This medicine eases the chills and fever of malaria.

For centuries people have put *sphagnum,* or peat moss, on cuts. During World War II, the moss was sterilized to kill germs and then made into pads. Doctors found that wounds covered with these pads healed much more quickly than those covered with cotton bandages. This is because the moss contains disinfecting substances that kill germs.

Even antibiotics (drugs that kill bacteria) have been used for many years. Over 3,500 years ago, Chinese doctors found that dressings containing *mold* worked very well in curing boils. But they didn't know why. Not until 1929 was this question answered. By accident Sir Alexander Fleming noticed that bacteria did not grow on his experiments if mold was present. He then found that the blue-green mold, like the kind that grows on spoiled oranges, made a substance he called penicillin. Penicillin, an antibiotic, still was not used for about 10 years after it was discovered. It was a success in treating wounds during World War II and saved many lives. Now about 40 antibiotics are used. All of them come from plants. Some common ones are streptomycin, aureomycin, and terramycin.

Many plants have been used for hundreds of years to treat cancer, which kills many people. Some of these folk remedies are over 3,500 years old. The plants are being studied to see if there are any that modern science can use. Some of these plants are periwinkles, yeast, autumn crocus, mistletoe, cucumbers, juniper trees, and American mandrake.

What Is An Animal?

ANIMALS LIVE IN all parts of the world. They swim in the water. They walk or crawl on the land. They fly through the air. Some animals, like tigers, lions, elephants, snakes, giraffes, and bears, are wild and live in the jungles and forests. Some animals are tame, or *domestic,* and live on farms, like cows, chickens, pigs, horses, and sheep. Other domestic animals, like dogs, cats and hamsters, live in homes with people.

To most people, animals do not look as much alike as plants do. There seems to be a huge difference between a fly, an elephant and a boy or girl!

Still, except for the tiny, one-celled plants and animals, it is fairly easy to answer the question, "How is an animal different from a plant?"

One big difference between animals and plants is that *no* animal can make its own food inside its body. Animals have to eat plants or other animals.

Another important difference is that most animals can move around. Most plants must stay in one place.

Another very important difference between animals and plants is that animals can see, hear, taste, smell, and feel. These *senses* enable the animals to respond to things that change or happen around them.

Most animals also have a brain. The brain helps animals find food, fight or escape their enemies, and discover good places to live. People, of course, can use their brains to learn to count, speak languages, write books, and build cities and machines!

In lands with hot summers and cold winters, many plants die when winter comes. Most animals cannot live in both very hot and very cold weather either. They have several ways of solving the problem of cold weather. Some migrate—they go to a warmer place in the winter. Some hibernate—they sleep or stay very still for the winter in a warm hole in the ground or a tree or in caves. Some grow very thick hair for warmth.

Many of the birds migrate. The Arctic tern probably makes the longest migrating trip. It flies 22,000 miles each year, from the far part of North America to the southern tip of South America, and then back again.

Cold-blooded animals have no way of keeping their bodies warm when the air turns cold. When winter comes, they must either hibernate or die. Frogs, toads, and turtles hibernate. These animals eat a great deal of food, then dig deep down into the mud under rivers, lakes or swamps, and sleep for the winter.

Many warm-blooded animals hibernate, too. Chipmunks, bears, beavers, and woodchucks (groundhogs) sleep through the winter. Others, like foxes and squirrels, grow very thick coats of fur before winter starts. This keeps them warm during the cold months of the winter. Still others, like people, are smart enough to build houses to protect them through the winter.

Animals usually have more ways of protecting themselves from enemies than plants do. Some animals are colored or shaped to blend in with their surroundings. Still other animals are protected by armor, sharp claws, or teeth. A few animals are smart enough to figure out ways to outsmart their enemies.

Animals that live in forests are often striped or spotted, like the giraffe, tiger, zebra, and leopard. The sunlight shining through the leaves and branches of the trees makes light and dark streaks in the forest, and striped or spotted animals are harder to see.

Some animals change color to match the winter snow. Arctic foxes, weasels, snowshoe rabbit, and ptarmigans (which are birds of the Arctic) are white in the winter but dark in the summer.

A few animals can even change colors when their surroundings change. The summer flounder can make itself any shade of brown or gray. It can also change its patterns of color to match its surroundings. If it is swimming in a creek with pebbles on the bottom, the fish has large spots. If it is in a sandy place, it gives itself tiny spots.

The tiny tree toad changes colors too. If it is on a leaf or green stem, it is green. If it is on the bark of a tree, it is

brown. The color change does not occur as soon as it hops from place to place, however. It usually takes about an hour for the toad to change colors.

A chameleon changes its colors, but apparently not to match its surroundings. A chameleon changes color because of excitement, light, and temperature. When it is in the bright sun, it is brown. If it is asleep it is usually light green. It turns bright green when it is excited.

Some animals are shaped like something where they live. The walking stick, a brown insect that lives in trees, looks like a twig. You have to look very closely to notice it.

The dead-leaf butterfly's wings have brown undersides. When it folds its wings together this butterfly looks like a dead leaf hanging from the branch.

One animal even decorates itself to look like its surroundings. The spider crab sticks tiny animals and bits of seaweed to its back and legs. It changes these when it moves to a new place.

If you see some strange living thing and you wonder if it is a plant or an animal, ask these questions:

Does it eat plants or animals? If it does, it is probably an animal.

Can it move from place to place? If it can, it is probably an animal.

Can it see, hear, smell, taste and feel? If it can, it is definitely an animal.

Does it protect itself from enemies? If it does, it is probably an animal.

Animal Families

THERE ARE ABOUT two million kinds, or *species*, of animals in the animal kingdom. All these animals are divided into two large groups. One group is called *invertebrates*, which are animals without backbones. The other group is called *vertebrates*, which are the animals with backbones.

Although the animals without backbones are much smaller and less familiar, there are many more of them. They are about 95 per cent of all the animals on earth.

Tiny one-celled animals like the ameba and paramecium are in the large invertebrate phylum *Protozoa*.

Another group of animals without backbones is the *sponges*. All sponges live in the water. Most of them live in the ocean, but there are some fresh-water sponges. Sponges are one of the few animals that do not move, and for many years people thought they were plants. (If you have a "sponge" in the bathtub, it might be the tough fibers of a sponge's skeleton. But probably it is plastic, and not a real sponge.)

Many of the animals that belong to the group *Coelenterata* also look more like plants than animals. Some of these are corals, sea fans, sea anemones, and jellyfish. All live in the water. Some move around to catch food. Others stay in one spot and capture food that floats past them.

Other ocean animals are members of *Echinodermata*. Their name means "spiny-skinned," and they are spiky animals like the starfish.

There are three groups of *worms* among the invertebrates. These are the flatworms, roundworms and segmented worms. They live in many different places—in

the soil, in the water, and inside other animals. Round-worms and flatworms are often parasites that cause diseases in people and animals. The common earthworm, which is helpful to man, is a segmented worm.

Another phylum of invertebrates is the *mollusks.* They are often called *shellfish,* because many of them have hard shells, but they are not fish at all. Clams, oysters, and snails, which have shells, are mollusks. But so are squids and octopi, which have no outer shells. All these mollusks are important as food.

Most of the animals on land, in the air, and in the sea are invertebrates called *arthropods!* Their name means "jointed feet." Since there are so many arthropods, they are divided into smaller groups called *classes.*

Probably the largest and best known class of arthropods is the *insects.* There are more than 800,000 kinds of insects. Not only are there many kinds of insects, but each kind produces many thousands of offsprings. For every person on earth there are probably about one million insects. Insects live in more different places than any

other animal. There is no place on land where they do not live. Many live in fresh water. Some even live in the ocean.

Many insects change as they grow up. When these insects are young, they look like worms. But these *caterpillars* grow into colorful butterflies or moths.

Other arthropods are *arachnids*. Spiders are members of this class. It is wrong to call spiders "insects," for all insects have six legs while spiders have eight. Spiders are meat-eaters, and they spin webs as traps to catch other insects to eat.

Crustaceans like shrimp, lobsters, crabs, and crayfish are another class of arthropods. Since these animals are covered with a very hard covering (like a shell), they cannot grow larger without shedding it.

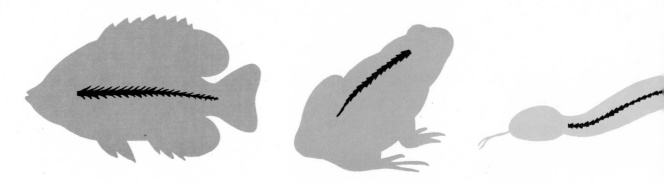

The centipedes (or "hundred legs") and millipedes ("thousand legs") are arthropods too. These names are not really correct. Some centipedes have over 300 legs, but no millipedes have as many as 1000 legs.

There are five main groups of animals with backbones: fish, amphibians, reptiles, birds, and mammals. All the animals in these groups have backbones made of separate small bones called *vertebrae*. They also have other bones in their bodies that make up the skeleton, or frame, that gives them a shape.

Some vertebrates are *cold-blooded animals*. Their temperatures change with the temperature around them. Fish, amphibians, and reptiles are cold-blooded. The other two groups—birds and mammals—are warm-blooded. Birds and mammals are able to keep a constant body temperature no matter what the temperature around them may be. (Your temperature stays at about 98.6 degrees whether the temperature outside is 10 degrees below zero or 110 degrees above—but a fish's temperature will change in hot and cold water.)

The group of animals called *fish* have to live in the water. Many special features allow them to live there successfully. They have *gills* for breathing, which take

oxygen from the water. A few fish also have lungs as well as gills. They can breathe out of the water as well as underwater.

Fish can move quickly through the water because they have very streamlined bodies. They have fins to steer and keep their balance in the water.

Most fish have scales, which get bigger as the fish grows. A baby fish has just as many scales as it will have when it is old. As the scales grow, rings form on them. Scientists can tell the age of a fish by counting these rings.

Amphibians usually live near fresh water or swamps and marshes. Their name comes from Greek words that mean "double life." Amphibians start their lives in the water and then spend the rest of their lives on land.

When they first hatch, most young amphibians do not even look like their parents. Young frogs, called tadpoles, breathe with gills, have no legs, and swim by moving their tails. As they grow, they lose their tails and gills and develop legs and lungs. They move from the water where they were hatched, and live the rest of their lives as land animals. Toads and salamanders follow this pattern, too.

Most *reptiles* live on land all their lives. Some, like the sea turtles, water snakes, alligators, and crocodiles, do spend much of their time in the water. They always lay their eggs on land, though, and their babies are hatched there.

All reptiles have dry scales on their skin. People who think that snakes are wet and slimy are wrong.

Scientists think that *birds* developed many millions of years ago from the reptiles. The scaly skin on their feet is very much like a reptile's skin. Birds are, however, very different from reptiles in several ways. They are warm-blooded animals. All birds, and only birds, have feathers. Birds also have true wings.

Some birds, like the blue-winged teal ducks, can fly 90 miles an hour. Other birds, like ostriches, kiwis, and emus, do not fly at all.

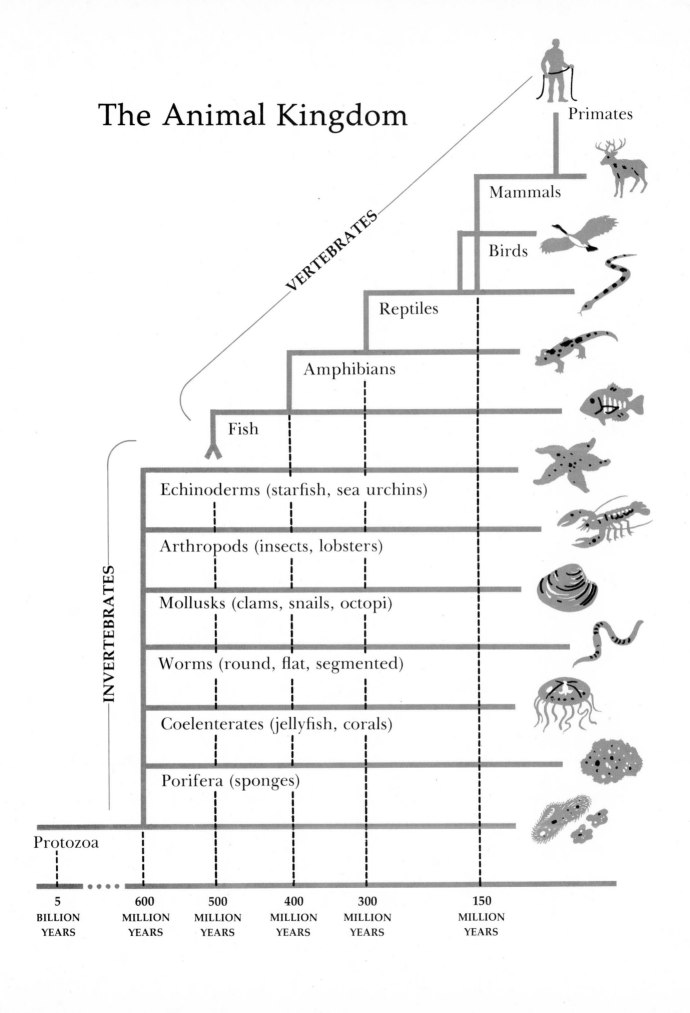

The Animal Kingdom

Primates

Mammals

Birds

VERTEBRATES

Reptiles

Amphibians

Fish

Echinoderms (starfish, sea urchins)

Arthropods (insects, lobsters)

Mollusks (clams, snails, octopi)

INVERTEBRATES

Worms (round, flat, segmented)

Coelenterates (jellyfish, corals)

Porifera (sponges)

Protozoa

5	600	500	400	300	150
BILLION YEARS	MILLION YEARS	MILLION YEARS	MILLION YEARS	MILLION YEARS	MILLION YEARS

Birds have no teeth and cannot chew their food. Instead they have special stomachs called gizzards. Birds swallow tiny pebbles that are used in the gizzard to grind up food.

The most intelligent group of animals is the *mammals*. This name comes from the mammary, or milk glands, that all mammals have to feed milk to their young. All mammals also have fur or hair. They are warm-blooded and breathe all their lives with lungs.

There are many different kinds of mammals, from people to whales.

Some, like cows, horses, elephants and hippopotami, eat grasses and plants. They are *herbivorous*. Others eat meat, like lions and tigers and dogs and cats and wolves. They are *carnivorous*.

Mammals live in many different places too. The strange-looking bat is a flying mammal. Whales and porpoises live in the sea like fish but they are mammals and not fish.

What scientists call "higher" animals are more complicated in the way their bodies and their nervous systems are built. Mammals have larger and more complicated brains than any other animals. These larger brains have helped mammals to survive while bigger animals, like the dinosaurs, have died out.

Ancient Animals

ANIMALS LIVED ON EARTH millions of years ago—long before there were people. Naturally, we have no descriptions or pictures of the ancient animals. To find out what those ancient animals were like, scientists study fossils. Fossils help us to know what the animals looked like and how many years ago they lived.

Some fossils are animals' footprints left in soft clay that later hardened into stone. Other fossils are bones, horns, tusks, or teeth of animals. Sometimes men find a whole animal preserved in ice, in stone, in tar, or in hardened resin from trees.

One fossil we have found is an armored fish called the *dinichtys*. Even though it was about 20 feet long, it moved very fast. It had jagged jaw bones instead of teeth. Since its jaws were very strong, it would snap its mouth shut with great force when catching a fish. For some reason, this fish died out while fish more like those of today continued to live.

The dinichtys lived in the Age of Fishes, 400 million years ago. Life on earth then was very different

from today. There were no plants on the ground. There were no animals roaming the land or flying in the air. There were plants and animals only in the sea. Even they were not like the ones living today.

About 300 million years ago, some of the water in the great oceans dried up. Land that had been under the water began to emerge. Plants slowly started to grow on the land. Now there was food so that animals could live on land, too.

Some fish slowly changed so they were able to breathe air and walk on the ground. These were the early ancestors of the amphibians. The Age of the Amphibians began.

Even the amphibians that live today start their lives from eggs hatched in the water. The young amphibians breathe with gills as fish do. As they grow up, they develop lungs for breathing air and legs for walking on the ground.

All the ancient amphibians lived near the water's edge. One was called the Eryops. It was about 8 feet long and looked like a huge frog with a tail. It had a very big mouth with very sharp teeth. It lived near swamps and ate fish and giant insects.

More than 200 million years ago some of the amphibians slowly began to change. They began laying eggs with hard coverings that did not need to hatch in water. These new animals were called *reptiles*. They lived on the land all their lives, and so no longer had to stay near the water.

For about the next 140 million years, reptiles ruled the land. This period is known as the Age of Reptiles,

or the Age of Dinosaurs, for that is another name for the land-dwelling reptiles. Some dinosaurs were giants almost 90 feet long, but there were many very small ones.

Most of the earth was tropical then. The land was low and flat with swamps and slow-moving rivers. Gentle rolling hills formed uplands. There were many vast green jungles of primitive plants. The temperature was warm all year round. Many huge dinosaurs lived in the swamps and ate the plants that grew there.

Brontosaurus had a very long neck and tail. Though it was 75 feet long and weighed 35 tons, it had a very small head. Its brain was about the size of a grapefruit.

The Diplodocus was about 90 feet long, but it was very slender and probably weighed only about 15 tons!

56

Scientists think that this huge animal ate about 500 pounds of plants each day.

Water was very important to these dinosaurs. When they were hungry, they would gulp down mouthfuls of water which was filled with tiny green plants. The water in the swamps also buoyed up their huge bodies. They were able to escape enemies by wading out to deep water.

Some dinosaurs ate meat, and so were enemies of the plant-eating swamp animals. The fierce, sharp-toothed Allosaurus lived in the uplands, but came down to the swamps for food. The Allosaurus walked on its hind legs, using its 18-foot tail to help it keep its balance. The short front feet of this dinosaur almost never touched the ground. They were used for fighting and holding food.

Some reptiles went back to living in the sea. Some of these creatures looked more like fish than reptiles, but they had no gills, and had to breathe air.

One of the strangest looking animals in the sea was the Plesiosaur. It looked like a snake stuck through the body of a turtle. The Plesiosaur swam with its long neck sticking way out of the water. When it spotted a fish, it would quickly duck its head underwater and catch it.

As years went on, the surface of the earth continued to change. Mountains formed and some of the swamps dried up. There were fewer plants for the swamp dinosaurs to eat, and so dinosaurs like the Diplodocus, Brontosaurus, and Allosaurus died out. More dinosaurs, however, appeared to take their place.

A carnivorous dinosaur even bigger and fiercer than Allosaurus ruled the land about 70 million years ago. This was Tyrannosaurus Rex (whose name meant "King

of the Tyrant Lizards"). It was about 47 feet long and
stood about 20 feet high. It looked very much like the
Allosaurus. Tyrannosaurus attacked using both its long
teeth and its short front feet and claws.

The plant-eating dinosaurs developed different ways
of protecting themselves against Tyrannosaurus and the
other meat-eating dinosaurs.

Stegosaurus had armor with two rows of tall upright
plates along its back. It also had four or more long spikes
at the end of its tail. Its tiny brain probably weighed
only 2½ ounces, and it had a second "brain" that was 20
times larger to control the big muscles of the tail and
hind legs. This second "brain" was really just a large
swelling of the nerves in its hip.

Another armored dinosaur was the Triceratops. It
was about 10 feet tall, and carried all of its defenses on its
head. It had a very wide bone that came out like a collar
to protect the neck from attack. It also had two long
horns over its eyes, and a short horn just above the nose.

Though Triceratops was usually very peaceful, it could charge and ram its sharp horns into even the fiercest attacking dinosaur.

There were reptiles in the sky, too. The Pterodactyls had wings like bats do today. Though some had a wing-spread of 25 feet, they were no heavier than a modern turkey. Some flying reptiles were as small as songbirds.

The earth continued to change. More mountains formed. More swamps dried up. The climate became cooler. The dinosaurs and the flying and swimming reptiles disappeared. No one knows why. Maybe the drying of the swamps killed the plants that the plant-eaters needed to live. With these animals gone, there was no food for the meat-eaters, and so they died too. Perhaps since dinosaurs did not stay to protect their eggs, other animals ate them, and so fewer and fewer baby dinosaurs were hatched.

Perhaps dinosaurs disappeared because the climate became cooler. Reptiles are cold-blooded animals. This means that when the climate became colder, the dinosaurs' body temperature lowered. If it became too cold, they died.

Some other kinds of reptiles, such as snakes, crocodiles, lizards, and turtles, continued to live. When the dinosaurs died, the mammals started to rule the land. The new period—the period in which we are still living— is the Age of Mammals.

A few mammals were on the earth during the Age of Reptiles. They were about the size of mice and usually came out only during the night. Over the years many different sizes and kinds of mammals appeared. Some of the early mammals that either changed or died out were the eohippus, the mastodons, and the mammoths.

The eohippus was a tiny horse that lived about 50 million years ago. It was about the size of a small fox and lived in the swamps. As the swamps dried up, it slowly changed. It grew taller and developed hoofs. Slowly it changed into the horses of today.

The mammoths and mastodons lived during the Ice Age about 50 thousand years ago. They looked very much like our elephants of today except they had long shaggy hair. Scientists know exactly how mammoths looked because whole animals have been found frozen in ice fields in the far north. No one really knows why the mammoths and mastodons disappeared, since their elephant relatives continued to live.

The Age of Mammals has been fairly short, compared with the Age of Fishes, the Age of Amphibians, and the Age of Reptiles. But probably mammals will continue to rule the earth for a long time to come. Mammals

have teeth to protect themselves, and hair to keep them warm. Most mammals take care of their babies until the babies are able to get along by themselves.

Many changes have taken place over the past 400 million years in the earth's surface and climate, and in the plants and animals that live on the earth. Changes are still taking place. These changes happen so slowly that we do not notice them. But even today the earth's animals—including humans—are slowly changing.

Smallest Animals

THE SMALLEST AND SIMPLEST animals, like the smallest plants, are *one-celled*. Their division or phylum is called the *Protozoa*. Probably they are one of the oldest forms of life on earth.

There are about 30,000 different types of protozoans! Most of them are too small to be seen without a microscope. They all thrive on moisture. Many live in water. Others live in damp soil. Some are parasites—they live inside the bodies of larger animals. Certain parasitic protozoans cause disease both in man and in other animals. African sleeping sickness, amebic dysentery,

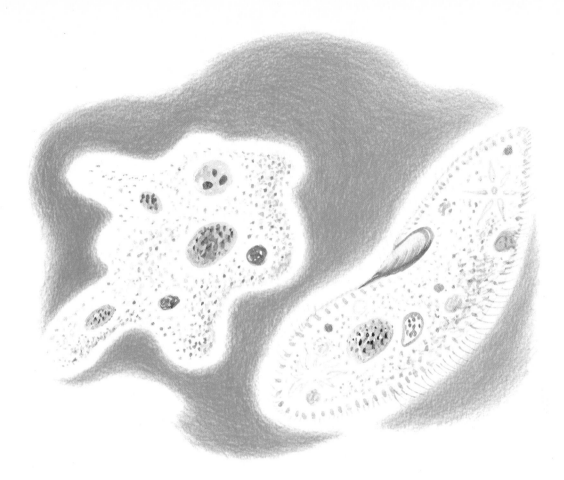

and malaria are some of the serious illnesses caused by tiny protozoans.

The *amebas* are tiny bits of shapeless jelly-like protoplasm with a dark spot in them. Almost all are too small to see without a microscope. Their one cell has to be able to do everything. When amebas move, part of their protoplasm flows forward to form "false feet." The rest of the cell follows along. To take in food, the ameba just surrounds it. To get rid of waste material, it flows away from it. And to make new amebas, the cell simply splits in two!

The *paramecium* is a protozoan shaped like a slipper. It moves by means of tiny "hairs" called cilia, which act like the oars of a boat. The cilia are also used to move food into the cell. Unlike the ameba, the paramecium's basic shape never changes.

The world's smallest *mammal* is probably the pigmy shrew. It is a tiny creature that weighs about as much as a penny and is only 3 inches long, including its 1-inch-long tail. A full-grown pigmy shrew looks very much like a tiny baby mouse. Shrews have to eat almost constantly to stay alive. They use up food so quickly because they are very active. In fact, few people have seen shrews because they move so fast. The tiny shrew in the picture is the same size as a real pigmy shrew!

The smallest *bird* is the hummingbird. These tiny birds are usually less than 4 inches from the tip of their bills to end of their tails. The hummingbird is built so that it can feed on the sweet nectar of flowers. Since the flowers would break even under a small weight, the hummingbird does not stand on the flower. Instead it beats its strong wings 55 times a second and hovers in the air like a tiny helicopter. It is also the only bird that can fly backwards.

Even though the hummingbird is so tiny, it is able to fly all the way across the Gulf of Mexico without stopping to eat or rest!

Biggest Animals

EVEN THE VERY BIGGEST animals are not as big as the biggest plants. Animal sizes are limited — most animals of a certain kind can get only so big, no matter how much they eat. Many plants, though, just go on growing and growing.

The *largest* animal is the blue whale. Whales are mammals even though they live in the ocean. These big whales are bigger than any land animal could be, because the water supports their weight. If a whale is washed up onto the shore, its lungs are usually crushed by the weight of its huge body.

The largest blue whale ever caught was 113½ feet long and weighed 340,000 pounds. It would take over 2,000 men to add up to that weight.

Even baby blue whales are much bigger than land animals. They are 23 feet long when they are born—and they grow very fast! In order to grow as big as grown-up whales, they have to eat a great deal. For seven months after it is born, a baby whale drinks about a ton of rich milk a day. By the time the baby no longer needs milk, it is usually more than 50 feet long. Until it is about 12 years old, a young whale gains about 90 pounds a day. It eats about 6,000 pounds of food a day when it is in the cold Antarctic waters where there is much plankton.

Although blue whales are huge, they eat only plankton and krill. Plankton is made up of tiny floating specks

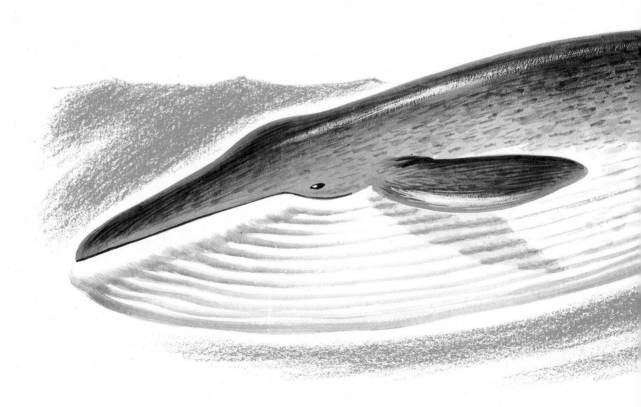

of plants and animals. Krill are tiny shrimp-like animals about 2 inches long, which live at the surface of the ocean and feed on the plankton. One whale eats about 1 million pounds of krill a year! One meal may include a ton or more of krill, plankton, and small fish.

The biggest animal that lives on the land is the African elephant. A grown elephant usually weighs about 6 tons and is 11 feet tall. The largest elephant we know about weighed 12 tons (24,000 pounds) and was 13 feet tall. Even the elephant's ears are huge. They are often 5 feet long and 4½ feet wide.

An elephant eats only plants. To get all the food it needs, it eats nearly all day long. The elephants in zoos and circuses eat about 500 pounds of hay and drink about 60 gallons of water a day.

A newborn baby elephant is 3 feet tall and weighs about 200 pounds. It is not fully grown until it is 25 years old. Scientists believe that wild elephants live about 50 years. One elephant lived in captivity in India for l30 years.

Giraffes are the *tallest* animals. Some grow to be 19 feet tall! Most of their height comes from their long neck (about 6 feet long) and their front legs (8 to 10 feet long). The giraffe's neck has very few bones and so it is not very flexible. A giraffe's neck has no more bones in it than a mouse's neck, or a baby's neck.

When the giraffe wants to reach the ground for food or water, it cannot simply bend its neck. It has to spread its forelegs wide apart and then stretch down, hardly bending its neck at all. So it is much easier for the giraffe to get its food from the top leaves of trees. It uses its 18-inch tongue and long upper lip to pull off mouthfuls of leaves. The giraffe gets most of its water from the leaves, and so it doesn't have to bend down to drink.

Baby giraffes are 5½ feet tall when they are born. They drink their mother's milk until they are about 9 months old and have grown tall enough to reach the leaves of trees.

Many people think that giraffes make no sound. Actually they make several sounds—from a low call to a hoarse roar. Young giraffes bleat like a little lamb.

Both giraffes and elephants are plant-eaters, or *herbivores*. The largest meat-eater or *carnivore* on earth is the Kodiak, or Alaskan brown bear. The Kodiak weighs up to 1,000 pounds and is 9 or 10 feet tall standing up. These huge bears usually hunt squirrels

and mice for food, but when the salmon migrate up the rivers, they eat all they can catch.

Ostriches are the largest living birds, but they cannot fly. An ostrich weighs about 300 pounds or more and is 8 feet tall! Ostriches cannot fly, but they can run very fast. An ostrich can run 50 miles per hour to get away from danger. Like all birds, it lays eggs—but an ostrich egg weighs about 3 pounds!

Natural Communities

JUST AS PEOPLE LIVE in towns, all plants and animals are members of some *natural community*. Just as a town has old people and young people and people with many different jobs, a natural community is made up of many different kinds of plants and animals.

Ecology is the study of how plants and animals live together in a community and how they depend on their surroundings and on each other.

The plants and animals who belong to a natural community keep what is called the "balance of nature." For instance, if all the animals in a community ate green plants, there would soon be no plants left. The natural community would not last very long.

What happens in a "balanced" community is something like this: A tiny insect eats some leaves from a green plant. Then a spider eats the insect. Next a small bird gobbles up the spider. And finally a large hawk captures and eats the smaller bird.

These links between plants and animals make a "food chain." The chain links together animals who eat different foods.

To keep the community balanced, the amount of food produced and the amount eaten must be about the same. Green plants *make* food in their leaves, using the sun to run their "food factories." All other living things, though, must get food from the green plants. So there must be more plants than animals in the community.

There are many kinds of natural communities in the world, because there are so many different kinds of living things. Biologists have divided the world into *biomes*—large areas where the weather, the land, and the plant and animal communities are much alike.

Many things affect the biomes. The kind of land, the soil, the rainfall, the temperature, the growing season, and the wind are all very important. They determine what kind of plants will grow in the area. The plants in turn determine the kinds of animals that will live there, since animals eat the plants. Each biome has its own way of life.

Tundra

THE *TUNDRA* IS IN the far northern parts of North America, Europe, and Asia. It is between the northern forests and the land where there is always snow. Most of the tundra land is flat.

Tundra is a Russian word that means "marshy plain." Except for the top few inches, the ground of a tundra is always frozen solid, and so the melted ice and snow cannot soak into the ground. They stay as ponds, lakes and marshes during the summer.

Tundras have very severe winters which last for about nine months of the year. The sun hardly shines

at all in mid-winter. The weather is very cold. In some places it gets as cold as 90° below zero. The ground often freezes as deep as 1,200 feet. There is some snow in the tundra, but the wind sweeps the snow away from the ground in many places.

No big trees grow in the tundra because the ground is frozen. There is not enough water for the roots. The plants in the tundra are small, and cling very close to the ground.

Summer in the tundra lasts from May to July. The sun shines day and night. During this time, the plants have to make enough food to last a whole year. In June the tundra is blanketed with gorgeous, blooming flowers. Plants grow almost everywhere.

About 900 different kinds of plants grow in the tundra. The most common ones are mosses, lichens, shrubs, wildflowers, and grasses. Perhaps the most important tundra plant is the lichen, which can grow all year round. In the winter, lichen is the only food available for some animals.

Many animals live in the tundra. Even during the coldest winters, there are the Arctic fox, the snowshoe hare, the polar bear, the musk ox, and the ptarmigan, a bird that even has feathers on its feet to keep it warm.

The large musk oxen roam the tundra in herds. They have very thick coats of fur to keep them warm during the winter. A musk ox can find plants to eat even under a layer of snow. The largest and strongest animal in the tundra is the polar bear. It usually finds a warm den and hibernates for most of the winter.

In the summer, the tundra is very busy with animal life. Many animals that left the tundra during the winter return from these warmer places. Herds of reindeer and caribou return from forests farther south where they spent the winter. Many birds, such as ducks, Canadian geese, and swans, come to spend the summer in the many lakes and ponds of the tundra. Many insects live around the water and fly among the flowers during the short tundra summer.

Forests

VAST AREAS COVERED with trees are called *forests*. There are special ways of life in the forest, too. But not all forests have the same kinds of trees. In North America there are two main kinds of forests, *coniferous* and *deciduous*. In tropical lands nearer the equator there are *tropical rain forests*.

CONIFEROUS FOREST

In coniferous forests the main plants are cone-bearing trees such as cedar, spruce, Douglas fir, and pine

trees. These trees are sometimes called *evergreens* because the needlelike leaves stay on the branches all year.

Low plants like ferns, mosses, and spring wildflowers grow in the coniferous forests too. In many places, the trees grow so close together that the sunlight does not get through to many of the lower levels of the forest. Most of the small plants can grow only in open patches where the trees are thin.

DECIDUOUS FOREST

The other important kind of North American forest has trees that shed their leaves in the fall. Maple, beech, oak, ash, basswood, poplar, hickory, aspen and other broad-leafed trees are called *deciduous*. They grow in the mild, moist areas that have long growing seasons.

The deciduous forest is divided into layers. Each layer has its own type of plant and animal life.

The bottom layer is probably the busiest part of the forest. Tons of dead leaves, logs, twigs, and animals and their wastes fall to the forest floor. Yet there is only a very thin layer on the ground at any one time. This is because tiny plants and animals like bacteria, fungi, molds, worms, termites, and carpenter ants are working constantly to decay it.

Many animals burrow into the ground for shelter or for warmth during the winter. Some of these burrowing animals are snakes, moles, shrews, weasels, chipmunks, woodchucks (groundhogs), and skunks. Other animals that can be seen during a walk through a forest are deer, foxes, mice, raccoons, bears, squirrels, and rabbits.

Just above the forest floor is a layer of bushes and vines, where many insects, birds, and animals live.

The highest layer is the forest *canopy,* which is formed by the tops of the trees. The leaves of this layer get most of the sun's rays. Little sunlight can get through to the ground, and so the lower areas of the forest are cooler in the summer. There is more moisture there, and much less wind.

Many animals can be found in this high sunny part of the forest. Birds like hawks, owls, orioles, and warblers live up there. They eat insects that live in the canopy.

TROPICAL RAIN FOREST

There are millions of square miles of *rain forest* near the equator in hot, wet areas that never have a dry season. The plants that grow here are used to getting at least 80 inches of rain a year. The trees have broad leaves that fall only a few at a time, so that the trees are never bare.

Many people think that *jungles* are the same as tropical rain forests, but there are important differences. Jungles have many thick, low plants, and may be in either wet or dry areas.

In the rain forest the dense canopy formed by the tree tops holds the heat and moisture like a huge greenhouse. Plants can grow very, very large. Trees in a rain forest are usually taller than those of the same kind in other forests. Some grow 300 feet tall, about as tall as a 35-story building! Some important trees in the tropical rain forest are teak, cypress, mahogany, and balsa.

The canopy, or top layer, is higher than in other forests because the tops of the trees are 120 to 300 feet from the ground. This layer gets the most light and heat from the bright sun. Many animals live in these high treetops. Brightly colored parrots, macaws, toucans, hummingbirds, hawks, and eagles spend most of their time there. At night squirrel monkeys and red howler monkeys climb to the tops of these trees.

The next layer is the smaller trees—60 to 120 feet tall. Below them is the layer of sparse, young trees that are not over 60 feet high. Many animal acrobats swing and hang from the branches. Monkeys swing freely from one tree to another. Porcupines, squirrels, sloths, snakes, lizards, birds, and thousands of kinds of insects live in these layers where the food is very plentiful.

In the true tropical rain forest almost no sunlight gets through to the dark forest floor. Only a few scattered shrubs live there.

Larger animals live on the forest floor. The largest ones are tapirs, jaguars, and pumas. Huge snakes like the anaconda (a water snake), and the boa constrictor sometimes live on the forest floor, or lay curled around the low branches of trees. Other animals found on this bottom level are the turtles, lizards, toads, weasels, anteaters, giant armadillos, and small deer.

Since there is so little sunlight on the floor of a rain forest, many tropical flowering plants are forced to climb high to get into the sunlight. Lianas, or climbing plants, grow up the sides of the trees. Sometimes the stems of these vines are 2 feet around and 500 feet long. The flowers of most of these climbing plants dangle on long stems back into the lower layer, where the butterflies live.

Other flowering plants live high in the trees. Such plants do not have roots that go into the soil for water. These *air plants*, orchids, mosses, and ferns, attach themselves to the tree branches and climbing vines.

Grasslands

THE LAND BETWEEN the deserts and the forests is the *grassland* or *prairie*. Here there is not enough water for the big trees to grow, yet too much rain for deserts to form. There are hundreds of miles of grasslands in the western and midwestern United States and Canada, in the western part of Africa, in the *pampas* of Argentina, and on the *steppes* of Russia.

Soil and rainfall determine how high the grass grows. Where there is plenty of rain and rich soil, the grass may grow to be 4 feet tall. Short grass less than 2 feet tall grows in grasslands that are closer to the desert.

Grass makes the soil richer. The old roots and leaves die, and make the soil very rich in humus. As a result, much of the grasslands in the United States has been turned into farms. The area is often called a "bread basket" because wheat, corn, oats, and other cereal grasses are grown there instead of the tall grass that would grow there naturally. Sheep and cattle are raised on the shorter grass of the western prairie, where it is too dry for farm crops. Millions of these animals roam the range.

People have changed the natural community of the grasslands by planting crops and raising sheep and cattle.

A true grassland no longer exists in the United States. There are only a few patches of land that people feel is too rocky or not worth farming.

The wildlife of the grasslands has changed, too. Herds of buffalo used to roam the prairies. Animals like deer, elk, and antelope used to live there, too.

When hunters and farmers and settlers came, there were few trees to protect the animals. Many of the animals had to become fast runners to get away from danger. Jackrabbits can run about 45 miles per hour by taking leaps as long as 21 feet!

Other animals, like gophers and ground squirrels, burrowed under the ground for protection. Their burrowing also helped the soil by loosening the ground. Some animals, like the antelopes, buffalo, and prairie dogs, lived in large herds for protection.

None of these ways of protection worked very well after many people came to live and build farms and towns in the prairies. Not much natural wildlife is left in the grasslands of the United States.

Animals like mice, gophers, ground squirrels, jack rabbits, prairie dogs, coyotes, kit foxes, snakes, and turtles still make their homes in the grasslands. Many grasshoppers, crickets, and spiders live here too.

There have never been many kinds of birds in the grassland because there are few trees. The few birds that live here are those that live on the ground like bobolinks, meadowlarks, hawks, and grouse, or "prairie chicken."

Deserts

DESERT LAND IS too dry for many kinds of plants and animals to live. Most deserts get less than 5 inches of rain a year. Some parts of the desert go for as long as 10 years without rain!

Deserts usually have less rain, more wind, and higher temperatures than other places. When it does rain on the desert, it rains very hard. Gullies, dry stream beds, and valleys are quickly filled to overflowing, but the water soon disappears. The temperature in the desert can be as hot as 135 degrees during the day, and below freezing at night.

The desert plants adapt themselves to dry places in several ways. Some flowering plants that live only one season depend on rain for their water. These plants have a very short growing period. When it rains, the seeds sprout, the plant grows, and flowers bloom, and produce more seeds. Then the plant dies, leaving only the seeds to wait for the next rain.

Other desert plants have special leaves that do not allow moisture to escape, or they have places to store water. Most plants lose much water through their leaves, but desert plants cannot afford to lose much of their precious water. The thick wax coating of the creosote plant's leaves keeps water inside the leaves. Other plants save water by having small leaves or by growing leaves only after a rain and then losing them quickly.

Many plants have developed ways to store water. The cactus plants have thick stems like huge sponges which can hold large amounts of water. The giant, tree-like saguaro cactus has folds like an accordion that let the plant expand to hold more water when it rains. The barrel cactus and prickly pear cactus also store water.

When the rains come, the dry and lifeless-looking desert becomes a beautiful garden. There is nothing prettier than a desert in bloom. Seeds that have been lying in the ground for many years just waiting for water are now able to sprout. These plants produce flowers in a few short weeks. The grasses that have died, except for their roots, spring up and cover the ground. The cacti have beautiful, bright flowers. The bushes that lost their leaves during the dry spell grow new leaves. This lovely desert garden lasts for a few weeks after the rainfall.

The daytime traveler sees very little animal life, but there are many kinds of desert animals. Because they are easily killed by the heat, desert animals are seldom active during the day. At night when the temperature is much lower, the desert becomes alive with insects, coyotes, bobcats, foxes, jack rabbits, lizards, and snakes. They search for food and water which they get from plants or the morning dew.

During the day, however, many animals stay in burrows under the ground while others stay very quiet in the shade of stones, plants, or ridges in the sand.

Desert animals, like desert plants, also have several ways of getting along without much water. First, they stay out of the daytime heat to save water. They get most, or all, of their water from eating plants and other animals. The water-storing cacti provide water for animals who are brave enough to attack the sharp spines.

The kangaroo rat may have the most practical answer. It never drinks water, and its food is dry seeds that do not contain water. It is able to make its own water by combining the hydrogen and oxygen in the food it eats. This very unusual ability allows kangaroo rats to live in even the driest deserts.

Other desert animals are able to store water. The desert tortoise has storage sacs for water under its shell. It fills them when the plants it eats are high in moisture.

Camels live in the deserts of Africa, Asia, and Arabia. The camel does not really store water in its hump, but it does save water by holding it in its tissue and cells in a very special way. Most animals have a constant body temperature, and keeping a temperature the same all the time takes a lot of water. Camels can save water because their body temperature increases very slowly as the heat of the day increases. During the night, the camel gives off heat, so that its morning temperature is low. As the heat of the day increases, its temperature rises. The camel's body temperature varies more than 6 degrees (Centigrade), while the normal variation in people is less than one degree. This special ability allows the camel to go without water for as much as one week in summer, or two weeks in winter.

Fresh Water Communities

NATURAL COMMUNITIES are not found just on land. Lakes and ponds have communities of their own. Water plants of all shapes and sizes live under the surface. Some of the plants are attached to the bottom while others float along the surface of the water. These plants provide food for water animals such as snails, fish, and insects. The lakes and ponds are also favorite homes for waterfowl like ducks, geese, swans, flamingoes, and cranes. Land animals also come to the lakes and ponds to drink the water and to eat the birds, fish, or plants that live there.

Plants and animals that live in the water have very different living conditions from those on land. Water buoys up and supports their bodies. Water also absorbs and holds heat and cold, so changes in temperature do not occur as suddenly in the water as they do in the air.

There are usually three zones of plant growth in a pond or lake, just as there are layers of life in the forest.

Cattails, bulrushes, reeds, and marsh grasses are plants that live in the shallow water closest to the shore. Their roots are in the soil under the water. These plants are the homes for many insects like water scorpions, sow bugs, water boatmen, and water bugs. Moths come to this zone to lay their eggs in the flowers of the cattails. Simple plants like green and blue-green algae grow on the water-soaked stems of these plants.

Floating plants live in the middle zone, where the water is 2 to 5 feet deep. The beautiful water lilies are very common here. Probably more insects visit the waxy, sweet-smelling flowers of the water lily than any other kind of plant. Many animals live on the underside of the water lily leaf. Protozoa (tiny, one-celled animals), snails, sponges, and many insects live under the protection of its leaves. Insects and frogs sometimes lay their eggs here too. With so many animals living around the water lilies, great numbers of large insects like dragonflies come to feed on the young animals.

Many kinds of animals live in the middle zone. Many kinds of fish—sunfish, bass, pike, and others—like to hide among the plants here. Bullfrogs and green frogs stay underwater except for their heads. Painted turtles and spotted turtles come to the area to feed on the small animals that live on the plants.

If the center zone is open water, a floating mass of millions of microscopic plants and animals called *plankton* may be found. The green scum often seen on many lakes and ponds is really due to the green algae in the plankton. Plankton is a very important food for many of the larger fresh water fish.

Salt Water Communities

ALMOST THREE-FOURTHS of the earth's surface is covered by large bodies of salt water. Much is still unknown about the oceans. Man is now exploring the ocean depths just as he is exploring outer space.

Living in the ocean has many advantages. The water temperature stays about the same. A continual supply of food and minerals floats through the water, and so plants do not have to have root systems to absorb food from the soil. The water buoys and supports the weight of plants and animals. Water animals can be much larger than they could be on land. Water plants do not have to

have woody fibers (like stems or trunks) to support themselves as most land plants do.

All plants must have sunlight to make their food. Because light does not reach the deep places of the ocean, plants live only in the shallower, sunlit layers.

The most important plants and animals in the ocean are part of the *plankton*. About 99 per cent of all ocean plants are found in this floating mass. In the spring, hundreds of miles of ocean are covered with plankton. This area often looks yellow, green or brown, depending upon the color of the plants in the plankton. Such areas have been called the "meadows of the sea." Many animals swim to these areas to eat the plankton.

In the shallow parts of the ocean live the bottom dwellers. Both plants and animals live in this area where sunlight can reach all the way down.

The food supply in the ocean shallows is so rich that all an animal has to do is to open its mouth, and the food floats in. The only problem is that the animal has to find

94

a place to anchor itself, for this is a very crowded part of the sea. Some burrow into the ocean bottom like the sea worms and fiddler crabs. Others, like barnacles and sea anemones, live on top of the shells of other animals. Some like barnacles, sponges, and mussels attach themselves to rocks, boats, or pilings of piers. Many crabs, snails, starfish, and shrimp move about from place to place getting food.

Many kinds of plants live in the shallow water. Seaweeds do not have roots, but they attach themselves to rocks and sand by flat "holdfasts." Many of the smaller seaweeds are groups of millions of algae that make a fuzzy green slime on the rocks or other things that have been underwater.

In the open sea, the fish are the rulers of the ocean. They share the deep water with whales and dolphins, which are mammals, and squid and octopi, which are mollusks. The animals who survive here need speed, protective coloration, and very keen senses.

Many of the large fish can swim 35 to 50 miles an hour. The blue marlins are the fastest, but the sailfish and tuna also move very fast.

The color of fish is very important. Their backs are dark, the color of the deep, dark water below. Any enemy above them will have trouble seeing them. But their bellies or undersides are light, so they will blend with the bright sky above when an enemy looks up. In very deep water the fish are dark all over.

Some of the slower animals have other ways of scaring away their enemies or catching food. The blowfish simply blows up like a balloon when an enemy comes near. The spines that normally lie flat on its body point out, and the fish, looking very fierce, is usually left alone. Animals such as the squid, octopi, and sea hares blind their enemies by squirting "ink" into the water. The angler fish looks like seaweed, and it dangles a "worm-like" piece from its head. When a small fish swims over to eat the worm, the angler fish eats the unsuspecting fish.

The deepest parts of the ocean are still largely mysterious places where man is only beginning to explore. The fish in the deep, dark part of the ocean are very strange. They are all flesh-eaters since no plants live this deep. Most have huge mouths with long, needle-sharp teeth. One tiny monster can even swallow a fish bigger than itself because it has a stretchable stomach. Many creatures of the dark oceans glow, which gives them an even stranger appearance as they swim through the dark water.

All About You

The Miracle of You

FASTER THAN A SPEEDING BULLET . . . *more powerful than a locomotive.* . . . How many times have you heard those words? They describe Superman, of course, a make-believe man who has super powers.

Have you ever wished that you were Superman? Well, you *are*.

For nothing could be more super than your own body. It is not just one, but many miracles all wrapped up in a miracle covering. That covering is so strong that it can keep out water and cold and heat, yet weighs so little that you don't even know you're carrying it around. And if ever that covering gets a little rip in it, it closes itself just like new, almost as if a magician had said, "Presto, disappear!"

What is inside that magic covering is even more miraculous. Did you know that every minute billions and billions of very tiny living things are at work inside you? And inside them are even tinier parts that decide things like the color of your hair and whether you are a boy or girl!

Did you know that there are parts inside you which are stronger than the strongest bridge? The men who build bridges and dams and skyscrapers have been studying these parts for years trying to copy them.

Did you know that you have a movie camera inside you that puts to shame any camera in any store in the world? It takes thousands and thousands of pictures every day and gets each one ready in less than a second.

Did you know that you have a great furnace inside you that is even more super than a two-story-tall furnace which melts metal? And drums inside your head which are far finer than those of any musician? And a fantastic pump that never stops during your whole life?

Did you know that you have a vast intercom system inside you? It works so fast that all the telephones in the world seem slow next to it!

Did you know that these and other super things each came from one single little spark of something far, far too small for you to see?

So you have many things inside you that make a speeding bullet seem like a slowpoke and a powerful locomotive look like a weakling!

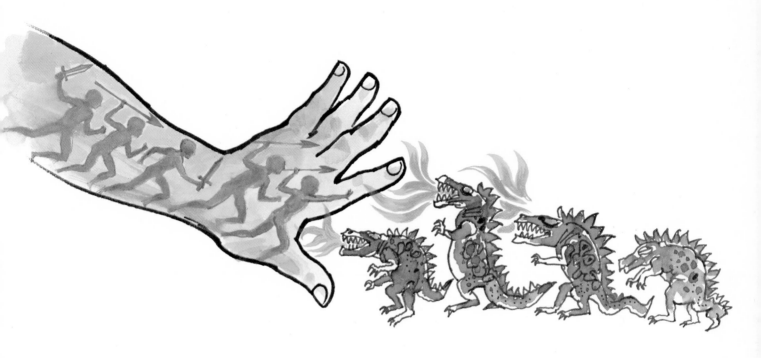

But you also have enemies that are always trying to get into your body and hurt these many super things that are yours. You have countless "soldiers" inside you to fight them, but the best way of all to keep out these enemies is by using your miracles in some *special* ways.

After finishing this book, you will know just what these special ways are. You will also know about wonders that are greater than any you have ever seen. Most of them are hidden inside you, so that until now you may not have cared a great deal about them. Also, because they are made by the most magical builder in the world, they work almost without your needing to pay any attention to them.

But they are there, and they are the most amazing things in the world.

Together, they are the miracle of you.

What You Are Made Of

THE MIRACLE OF YOU is a miracle of large parts that are stronger than steel or better than the best movie camera. But before that, it is a miracle of the smallest part of you.

This tinier than tiny part is what every living thing on earth is made of. No matter how different living things are from one another, all are made up of this part, though it is too small to see with your eyes.

A fish has it, an elephant has it, a bug has it. And you have it. In fact, you have billions and billions of these small parts inside you. They are *cells*.

Cells have many different shapes and jobs.

Nerve cells are long and slim with clusters of thin branches at the ends. Fat cells are round and . . . fat!

But some cells can *change* their shape. When muscle cells become stimulated, they get shorter to give you strength. Other cells can move like little cars. Whenever a sickness invades your body, for instance, certain cells rush from wherever they are to fight the sickness.

SOME OTHER CELLS

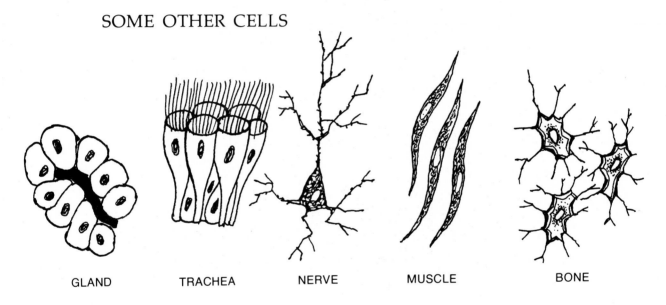

GLAND   TRACHEA   NERVE   MUSCLE   BONE

Cells also contain tiny parts that make *you* different from everyone else, from how tall you are to the lines on your hands.

Most cells can *make* things that the body needs, too. And even more important, all cells—except for the ones that make up your brain—can make *more cells*. To understand how cells do this, you must first understand the parts that make up these smallest parts of you.

First, all cells have a kind of skin around them, called the *membrane*. It is thin enough so that what the cell needs can enter through it, and what the cell must rid itself of can pass out through the membrane.

The main thing that the cells of your body need, of course, is "food." Their food comes to them through the blood as it moves through your body.

Inside, the cell is made of *cytoplasm*. In the cytoplasm near the middle of the cell is what looks like a large dot. This dark spot is the very important *nucleus*. The nucleus directs the cell. If a cell is cut in two, the part with the nucleus can fix itself and become whole again. But more often the cell cuts itself in two—right in the middle of its nucleus. The two parts move apart and become two new cells. They multiply by dividing!

All the parts of a cell together are called *protoplasm*. A group of the same kind of cells that do the same job is called a *tissue*. When different kinds of tissues then work with each other to do an even bigger job, they are named *organs*. Finally, a number of organs work together to form a *system* of the body.

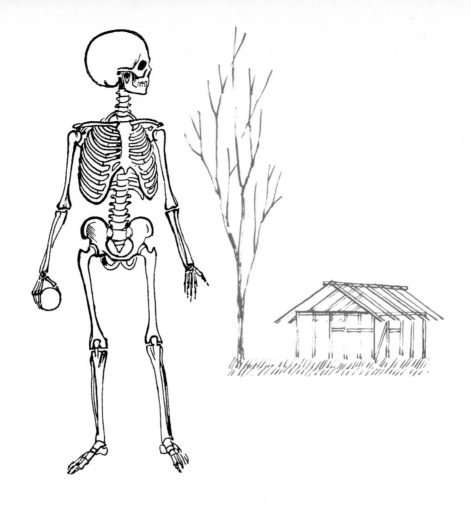

Your Framework

"PLASTIC MAN" OF THE comic strips was able to bend and stretch his body into any shape from an automobile to an ashtray. But in real life we have only one form. Some people are larger than others, but all of us have the same kind of *skeleton*, which is made up of 206 bones that do many different jobs.

Their first job is simply to hold us together and give us our framework. Without a skeleton, man would be just one large, jellyfish-like blob.

Another important purpose of bones is to protect the soft *organs* and *tissues* deep inside our bodies. Almost all of the 28 bones in the head or *skull,* for example, are there to protect the brain. They are called the *cranium,* and never move. The one bone in our skulls which does move is the lower jaw or *mandible.* If it didn't, we would not be able to speak or eat!

Most bones *must* move as well as protect. Our 24 ribs can move in and out so that the lungs they surround can expand when we breathe. *Movement,* in fact, is one of the most important jobs done by the bones. Every bone that we have (except one in the throat) meets with another at a place called a *joint.* These joints are "oiled" with a special fluid and when finally joined by muscle connected to our bones, allow the body a wonderful variety of motions, from the sweeping movements of an acrobat to the precise movements of a surgeon.

The most important "bone" in the body is the spine. The spine is actually made up of a number of hollow tubes called *vertebrae.* If your spine—or "backbone"— really were only one long bone, you would be much like a statue. You would never be able to bend your body or move your head. The one *vertebra* at the top of your spine lets you nod when you like something; the vertebra right below it lets you shake your head from side to side when you don't.

Firmly attached to each vertebra is a *disc* of strong but springy *cartilage,* one of the two materials that hold the bones to each other. In the beginning, all bones are cartilage. As you get older, calcium is deposited in them so that they harden.

The other material holding the bones is called a *ligament,* which is a thick cord of tissue. In the spine,

106

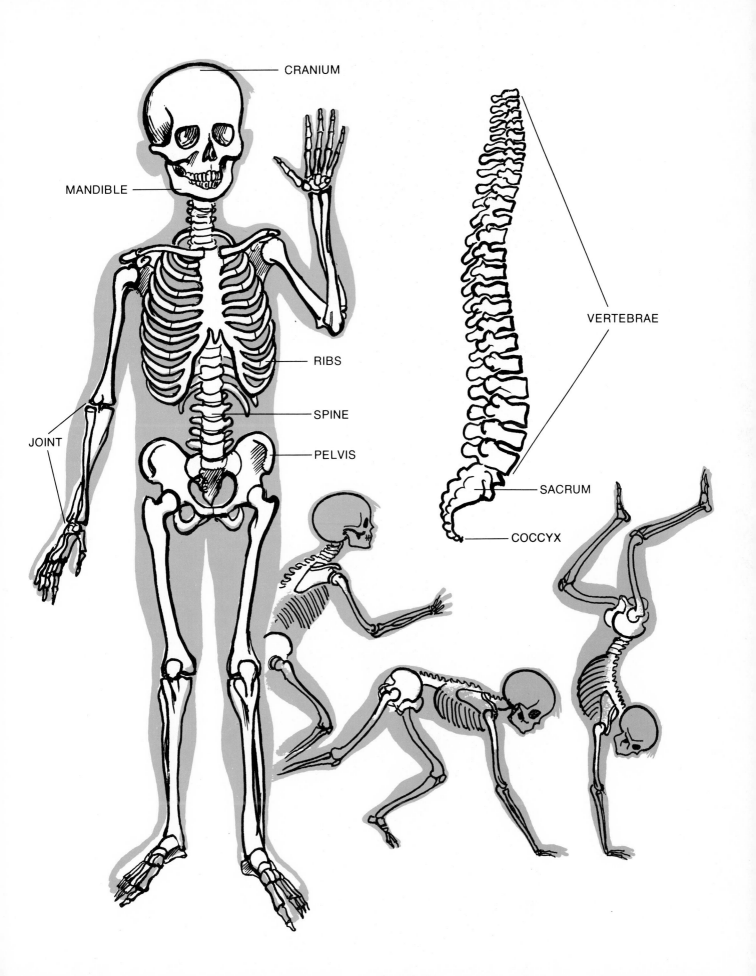

CRANIUM

MANDIBLE

JOINT

RIBS

SPINE

PELVIS

VERTEBRAE

SACRUM

COCCYX

these ligaments tie the vertebrae together so that they can move in all directions—even backward a bit—without having anything break or pop out of place.

As well as letting you move, the backbone protects the *spinal cord*, the bundle of nerves through which the brain sends out messages telling the body what movements to make. Fibers in the spinal cord also carry messages up to the brain from many parts of the body.

A child has 33 vertebrae in his spine, but as he gets older, some of these vertebrae grow together. An adult has only 26 bones in his spine. Near the bottom of the spine, several bones grow together to form the *sacrum*. At the very bottom of the spine, several bones become the *coccyx*, the only bone in the entire skeleton that is not used for anything.

Bones are long-lasting as well as useful. They can stand as much strain as steel, while only taking up a fifth of the body's weight. They are so strong and durable that they survive thousands of years, and from them we can tell what men looked like long ago.

One reason for their unusual lightness is that most bones are hollow inside. This helps to make them even stronger, just as a metal pipe is stronger than a solid metal bar. Inside most bones there is also a spongy *marrow*. Where fat is stored, it is yellowish in color. But in the parts of many bones, the marrow is reddish. This is because blood is made there—still another job done by our bones. All in all, bones are an amazing part of you.

Your Muscles

WITHOUT STRINGS OR A HUMAN HAND inside it, a puppet cannot move.

Your bones cannot move either without the human *muscles* which are their strings. But unlike a puppet's strings, your muscles are where you cannot see them, under your skin and inside your body. There are hundreds of them and they make up almost half your weight. The muscle in your thigh is almost two feet long and very strong. But the strongest muscle of all is the *masseter* muscle of your inner jaw. It has to be strong enough for you to chew beef—which is the muscle of cattle!

What is a muscle like? Have you ever seen the inside of a rubber golf ball? It has many, many rubber bands tightly locked together. The bunches of human muscle *fibers* look like this, only they are long instead of round.

The remarkable thing about muscles, however—and the thing that makes them different from everything else that is a part of you—is that muscle tissue can shorten or stretch. As the muscle shortens or stretches, it pulls the bones and makes them move.

Most muscles are thicker in the middle and thinner at the ends. When contracted, they become even thicker in the middle. This is why you see a little bump when you flex your *biceps*—the muscle in the front of your upper arm.

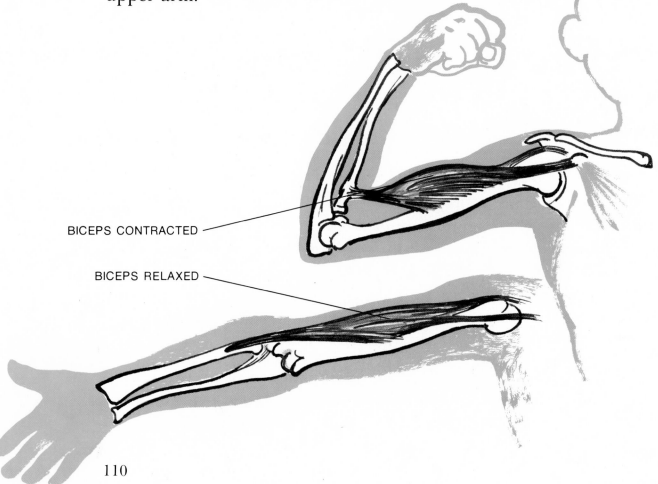

BICEPS CONTRACTED

BICEPS RELAXED

But the most interesting thing about a muscle is that, just as it teams up with a bone to let you move, it also teams up with another muscle at the same time. While you make a "V" with your arm to show your biceps, your *triceps*—the muscle on the other side of your upper arm—is relaxing. And when you open your arm, your triceps shortens to do the work while your biceps expands and relaxes.

Muscle is as amazing as its partner, bone. Whether you decide to frown or grin, to stand on your tiptoes or move a paint brush across a wall, your muscles are leaping into action within just a few one-hundredths of a single second. What's more, each muscle is ready to support a thousand times its own weight!

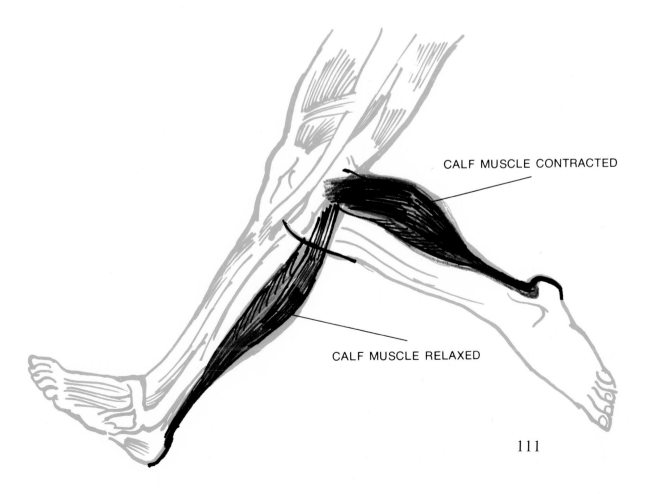

CALF MUSCLE CONTRACTED

CALF MUSCLE RELAXED

But most of the fibers of a muscle are usually not used when you do just easy things. It takes very hard work to call all the muscle troops into action. When this happens, however, then they must grow bigger and harder to do the task. Using the muscles you have is how you get real "muscles."

Developing your muscles changes the way you look. It is your many muscles which give you your exact shape in the first place. That's why a Mr. America winner looks a bit different than most other men. If you do not use them, your muscles shrink and weaken. Then, among other things, you will find that your teeth chatter more easily when the weather is cold. This is because your muscles do another job—they keep you warm, like a solid coat between your bones and skin.

These hundreds of muscles that you can use to make your bones move are called *voluntary* muscles because it is almost always up to you whether you want to use them. But there are also thousands of smaller muscles in your body called *involuntary* muscles. Except for a few people, like the sword swallowers who have practiced for years contracting their throat and stomach muscles, these *involuntary* muscles are ones over which you have no control. They are in many places such as the stomach, where they help digestion, and even the skin, where they pull the hair erect to cause "goosepimples."

Have you ever held a mirror before your eyes in a dark room and then suddenly turned on the light? If you do, you will see that the round center or pupil of your eye gets smaller because of the *involuntary* muscles controlling it.

INVOLUNTARY MUSCLES AT WORK

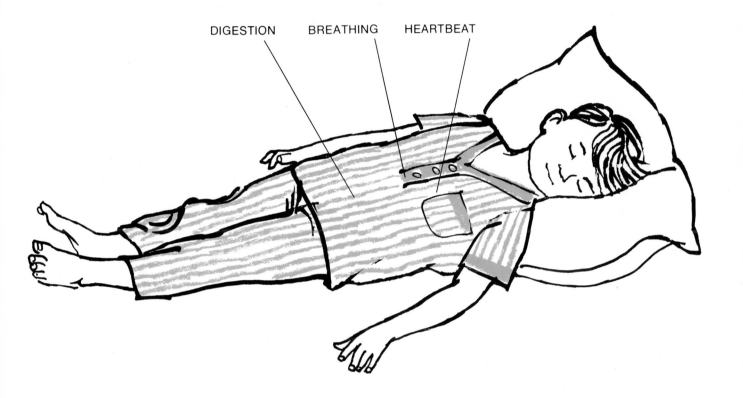

DIGESTION   BREATHING   HEARTBEAT

Muscles are very healthy because they are rich with blood. Any trouble that we have with muscles usually happens when they are not used enough, and do not move the blood about as much. You might think, then, that nature wanted to arrange the human body so that its most important part would be muscle that would always be in use.

This is just what nature has done! There is a special group of muscles within you that is in constant use all your life—your heart.

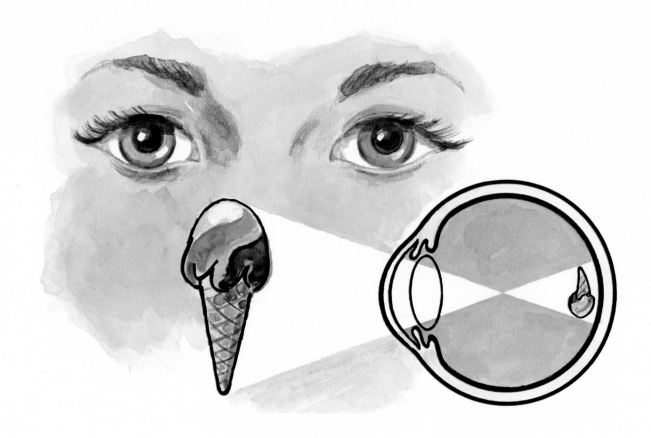

Your Eyes

HOW WOULD YOU LIKE to have the best movie camera in the world? It would be one that from morning till night would take moving color pictures more real than any camera in any store could take.

Well, you do have just such a camera—your eyes!

What you make your bones and the muscles do will depend a lot on what is going on outside you. And what you *see* tells you a lot about the world around you.

If you see this page, for example, it is a "stimulus" which your eyes "sense." Actually, before you can really see the stimulus, your eyes must send a message about

114

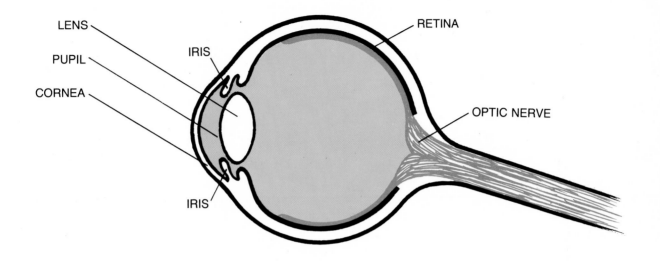

LENS

PUPIL

CORNEA

IRIS

IRIS

RETINA

OPTIC NERVE

it to your brain. How does it get there — and how do you "see" a picture of a page?

First, light rays bounce off the page and travel to your eyes.

Your eyes look pretty much like balls and are covered with a white covering that protects them. The part of your eye that shows is a transparent place in this covering called the *cornea*. The light passes from there through a watery fluid to the tissue which gives the eye its color, the *iris*.

In this iris is a circular hole called your *pupil*. Sometimes this hole is bigger than at other times. Muscles around the pupil make the hole smaller when light rays are bright in order to protect the sensitive inside parts of the eye. It is bigger in dim light to let in enough light to see by.

Now the light rays go through the pupil to the *lens*. The lens is a tiny but important disc which also can change size because of the muscles around it. This is what allows you to see things that are either close up or far away. The space between the lens and the cornea contains a watery fluid, while the rest of the eye is filled with a material that is like a clear jelly.

The light rays bouncing off the page travel through the lens, which bends them and puts the "picture" in focus on the back of the eye. The inner layer—which is like the film in a camera—is the *retina*. This is a super-sensitive tissue with nerve endings that go to the brain. Once the brain receives the "stimulus" of the page from the retina, it is *then* that you actually *see* this page.

Your eyes don't really see, in other words. Your brain does. But since your brain is "blind," locked inside of your head, it needs your eyes to send the messages from the outside world to it.

When you grow up, your eyes will be only about an inch across. Yet they do things for you that no camera in the world can do.

Your Ears

HAVE YOU EVER SEEN someone play a drum?

Well, you have a drum in each of your ears, and these drums help you hear all the sounds of the world, from the loudest explosion to the softest whisper. Your "eardrums" are not played by wooden sticks, but by air through which waves of sound are traveling.

These sound waves can come from many miles away, yet the two-inch journey that they make through your ears is their most amazing journey.

Your outer ear—the "ear" you can see—is called the *auricle*. It is really just a kind of funnel to collect the waves of sound moving toward you. Inside each auricle is an opening and a one-inch passageway into the skull called the *auditory canal.*

And here is your "eardrum" or *tympanic membrane,* a thin, tight tissue. This "vibrates" or moves back and forth very slightly but very quickly.

On the other side of your eardrum is a small space, the "middle ear." Inside it are three very small bones, connected in a special way to make sounds louder and then to pass them on to the "inner ear." The first bone touches your eardrum, and the last one touches a thin membrane in the spiral fluid-filled bone called the *cochlea.* The cochlea looks like a snail's shell and contains special cells and nerve endings that pass the vibrations on to the brain.

As you can tell, your ears work in much the same way as your eyes do. It is your brain that really "hears"— but it needs your ears to help it do so.

All in all, the ear is a pretty complicated thing. There is much more to it than a "drum." But when you stop to think that it must catch sound waves traveling faster than 10,000 vibrations a second, you can understand why nature made your ear the way it is.

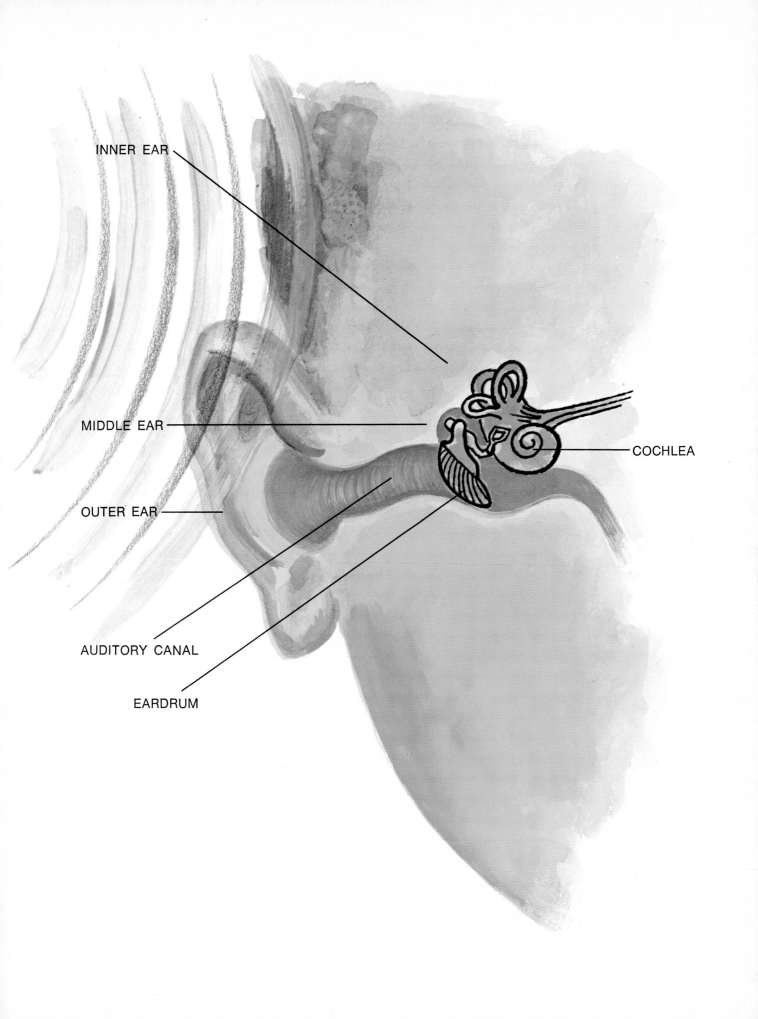

INNER EAR

MIDDLE EAR

COCHLEA

OUTER EAR

AUDITORY CANAL

EARDRUM

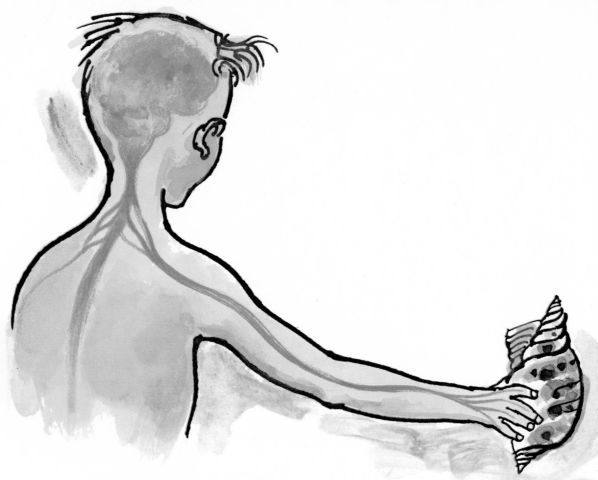

Your Sense of Touch

BEFORE YOU EVER SAW or heard anything, you felt loving arms around you. As you grow older, your sense of *touch* tells you many important things about the world. Man, in fact, is the only creature on earth who can tell what an object is by touch alone.

Touch is the sensation that you have when part of your body comes into contact with something outside of it. In your skin are *nerve* cells that carry the stimulus of whatever touches you to your brain. Then you "feel" it.

Different nerve cells tell you of different feelings. There are more than 15,000 cells, for example, that let you know whether something you touch is hot or cold. And there are *millions* that tell you of pain, since it is very important to know when something is hurting you.

The message which will go to your brain begins when something comes up against the little hairs that are all over your body, moving the tiny muscles next to them. This in turn awakens the nerve cells.

Some parts of the body are not as sensitive as others. The palm of your hand can tell much more about what it is touching than your elbow can. Your fingertips are the best "feelers" of all. This is because nature made your hands for touching and identifying things just as much as for holding them.

Just as your eyes can take in the entire scene around them, and your ears can hear each of the many sounds of a band or orchestra playing together, you can pick up a handful of sand and know right away that it is cool, damp, rough, and even filled with a few larger stones.

Your Sense of Smell

HOW DO YOU KNOW what is cooking on the stove for dinner when the lid is on the pot? How do you know that someone is burning leaves in the fall even before you see the smoke? How can you tell when your mother is wearing perfume?

The answer is another of your senses — *smell*.

Though the nose is meant for breathing, it is also made for smelling. It works like this:

The two holes in your nose — the *nostrils* — have a partition in between them called the *septum*. The lower part is cartilage. This means you can move the bottom of your nose back and forth. But you cannot move the top of your nose, since it is made of real bone.

High up in the back of your nose is a small space. In it is the tissue that senses smells—the *olfactory membrane*. As with your other senses, nerves near that tissue have to send its message to the brain before you actually *smell* the good soup boiling on the stove. These nerves are very close to your brain, of course, and need to take only a short trip.

Before they can send their message to the brain, you must "smell" something. That happens when your nose breathes in air with something a little different in it. You sniff. The odor is carried up, through thousands of small, mucus-covered hairs, to the olfactory pocket. A slice of a second later, you smell burning leaves.

Unlike your other senses, the nose cannot smell a number of odors at one time. So nature makes the olfactory cells so that they get used to an odor. After you smell the soup cooking on the stove for a few seconds, your nose will not react to it as much. Then you will be able to smell your mother's perfume better when she comes into the kitchen.

Many animals use their sense of smell even more than their eyes and ears. Human beings, however, use this sense much, much less. But there are times when smell can still tell you important things—as when that pot has been on the stove too long!

Your Sense of Taste

"A SPOONFUL of sugar helps the medicine go down."

Do you recognize that famous line from *Mary Poppins?* There is a lot of truth in it, for what we like to eat most often depends on how foods "taste" to us.

The sense of *taste* works much the same as our other senses. Very small clusters of special cells or organs—called *taste buds*—team with your brain to tell you whether something in your mouth is sweet or sour, salty or bitter. Other cells tell you whether food is hot or cold.

Like *smell,* your sense of taste does not play as large a part in your life as seeing or hearing or feeling. But there are times when taste can tell us things we could not know as well any other way. A tiny taste on the tip of your tongue can often tell you whether or not the food is spoiled. By taking a little taste of what a man drank or ate last, doctors and detectives can sometimes tell if he has been poisoned. And, of course, the taste of good food is the most enjoyable part of eating.

Yet it is not always that easy to tell what you are tasting. For example, if you eat a candy bar, its sweetness will change the taste of anything sour that you eat afterward. Also, some "tastes," like onions, are really smells. An old trick is to close your eyes, hold your nose, and eat a bite of apple and a bite of onion. Unless you cheat— and sniff the onion—chances are you will not be able to tell which is which just by the taste.

Once when you had a bad cold, perhaps you found out for yourself how important smells are in "tasting." Your cold did not really affect your taste buds at all. But your stuffy nose kept you from smelling what you were eating—and so you couldn't taste it either.

Several other things help out your sense of taste, too. Some nerve cells in your mouth and on your tongue tell you what the *texture* of food is. It may be crisp like bacon or smooth like ice cream. It may be crunchy like peanuts, soft like bananas, or juicy like oranges.

Still other nerve cells tell you whether the food in your mouth is *hot* soup or *cold* lemonade.

You can see that your sense of *taste*—the weakest sense you have—is helped out by many cells that sense both *smell* and *touch*. If you are drinking cocoa, for instance, you smell the chocolate first. You feel the warmth and the smoothness of the liquid. The only job that your taste buds have is to tell you that the cocoa tastes sweet.

Maybe this is why nature decided to give us only as many taste buds as we really need. When you were a baby, you had them all through your mouth, but when you grow up, your taste buds will be mainly in a few places on your tongue and throat. Slowly most of them will have disappeared without your ever knowing it.

The ones that remain are more than enough to let you know what you are tasting, because your taste buds have so many helpers. The buds on the tip of your tongue tell you about sweet things, the sides tell of salty and sour tastes, while the back informs you when something is bitter.

You also have a few taste buds inside your cheeks and on the roof of your mouth. But these places do not seem strange when you think of where the taste buds of some creatures are located. Fish have them on their skin!

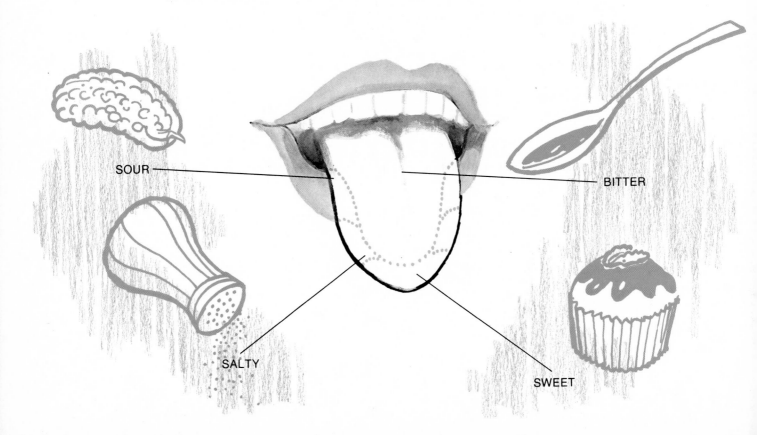

What Happens to Food?

LONG AGO, WHEN MEN KNEW little of what made up the world, some men tried unsuccessfully to change less valuable metals into gold. These were men called "alchemists." Little did any of them dream that the greatest "alchemist" of all was at work every day inside their bodies, taking some big chunks of food and making them into countless new tiny parts that their body needed to stay alive.

This "alchemist" is the *digestive system,* and it takes everything you eat, from milk to mushrooms, and turns them into *you!*

The cells of your body are fed and repaired by the food that you eat, which is brought to them by the blood. But of course things like carrots and hamburger, apples and eggs cannot be carried through the body as they are. They must be changed. *Digestion* is this change.

Digestion begins in your mouth, where the very first change is made in the food you eat—when you chew it into smaller parts. To make sure that you can chew any food, your teeth are covered with the hardest material in your whole body—*enamel.* Inside the enamel is another substance that is harder than bone—*dentine.*

The instant that food touches your taste buds, digestive juices called *saliva* in your mouth begin helping your teeth to transform it. Unlike the instant sensation of taste, though, the process of digestion is like a long-distance race which only begins in the mouth. The one kind of food which can be digested before you swallow it is called *starch.* But all the other things you eat must "run" the great "race" through your digestive system before they become ready for your cells.

Once the food has been cut, ground, and softened into pieces that you can swallow, it goes to one of two openings from the throat. The other leads to where you breathe. When you eat too quickly or talk when swallowing, some food may "go down the wrong way" and make you cough. But the place where your food almost always goes is to a long, narrow passage.

This is your *esophagus* and it has strong muscles that push the food down to your *stomach,* which stretches to make room for it. There what you ate is moved about while digestive juices pour into it from the wall of the

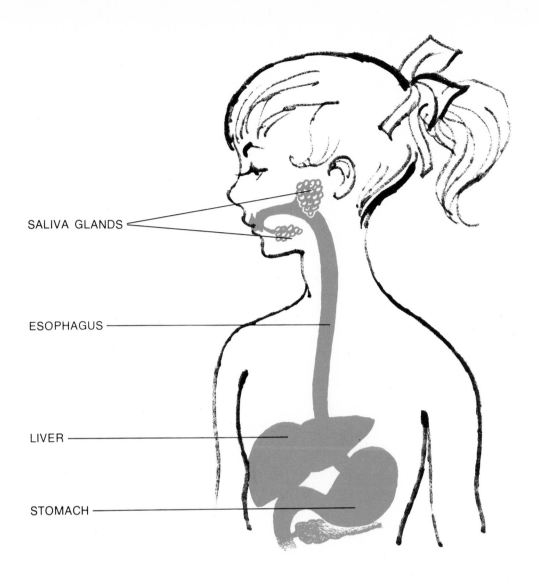

SALIVA GLANDS

ESOPHAGUS

LIVER

STOMACH

stomach. These juices are very strong, but they do not harm the stomach because it is protected by a special and very tough lining.

The next part of the great "alchemy" of digestion takes place when the food moves, a little bit at a time, into your *small intestine.* This tube is three times as long as your father is tall, and here is where the food finally gets ready to be used by the tissues of the body.

Along the way your *liver* (which also helps make blood) and *pancreas* send in juices to aid in digestion. What look like millions of tiny fingers, called *villi,* soak up the liquid "food" which now looks like anything but food. From the villi it goes to the blood and, finally, to your hungry cells.

The small intestine's muscles contract while the food is passing through. Their movement is called *peristalsis,* and it takes the food that is not used down into the *large intestine* or *colon.* Here it reaches the end of its race, passing out through the *rectum.*

Much of the unused food is in the form of liquid, however, and still must travel on. It is taken back into the system, for your body has several parts of liquid for every solid part, and needs its fluid.

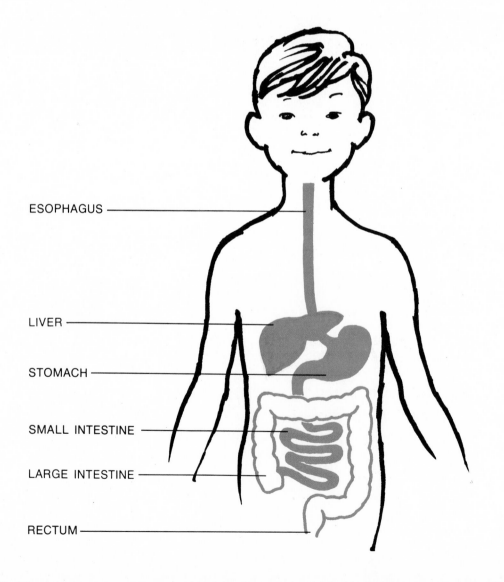

ESOPHAGUS

LIVER

STOMACH

SMALL INTESTINE

LARGE INTESTINE

RECTUM

Two large, bean-like organs, the *kidneys,* get rid of the fluid that you cannot use. Each kidney contains miles and miles of little coiled tubes. Blood flows through them and takes what it can use. The waste that is left over passes into a sac called the *bladder,* where it is stored. When the bladder gets fairly full, the liquid is emptied by the process of *urination.*

All in all, the "alchemy" of digestion takes a full day before it is completed. When the food that you put in your mouth twenty-four hours earlier is turned into *real* food for the billions of cells of your body, you are ready for another day of life.

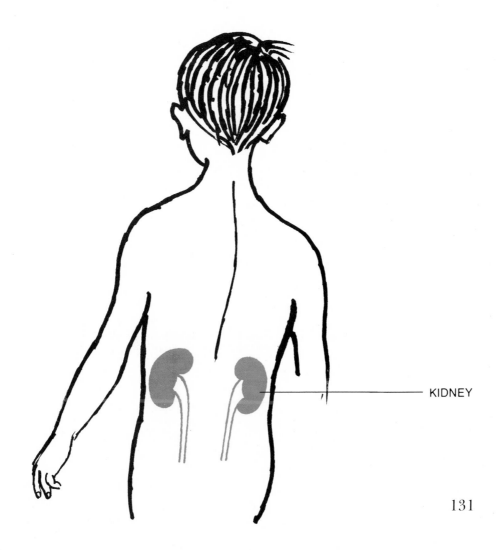

KIDNEY

What Should You Eat?

WHEN YOU GO TO a supermarket, you see shelves and shelves and shelves filled with all kinds of different foods. But the truth is that, as far as your body is concerned, there are only a very few kinds of basic foods—so few that you can count them on your fingers.

Two of those kinds of foods are called *carbohydrates* and *fats.* They give you energy, so of course you need some of them regularly. Good sources of carbohydrates are bread, macaroni, potatoes, sugar, and peas. Butter, bacon, cream, and vegetable oils are foods with a great deal of fat in them.

An even more important food element is *protein,* which is used to build new body tissue and to repair old tissue. Protein is broken down into what are called *amino acids.* They are not stored by your body, so it is important that you eat protein each day of your life. Meat, eggs, kidney beans, cheese, and milk are fine sources of this kind of food.

Your body also needs small substances called *vitamins,* which have letters for *their* names.

Vitamin A gives you healthy eyes and skin, and helps you grow. Some of the foods that contain it are egg yolk, liver, peaches, and carrots.

There are several vitamins named with the next letter of the alphabet and together they are called the *Vitamin B complex.* Vitamin B_1 aids your appetite, and can be found in pork and peanuts. Vitamin B_2, which helps you to digest carbohydrates, and Niacin, which gives you healthy skin, are found in lean meat, liver, green leafy vegetables, and whole-grain cereals.

Healthy gums and healing powers come from Vitamin C, which you can get from oranges, lemons, grapefruit, and strawberries. Vitamin D is needed to make strong teeth and bones. The best food sources of this vitamin are milk and eggs.

No matter how *much* food you eat, unless you eat the *right* foods your body will not get the proper vitamins. These right foods also give you a last important thing that human tissues require in very small amounts— *minerals.* Calcium, phosphorus, iron, sodium, iodine, and a number of other minerals help you live and grow. Like vitamins, each is found in many foods.

Just as there are only a few kinds of food elements, so there are really only a small number of foods that you need to eat to get your protein, carbohydrate, and fat, and your vitamins and minerals. If you have cereal, fruit, and eggs for breakfast, a fresh vegetable salad for lunch, and meat, potatoes, and milk for dinner, you will be eating most of the basic foods your body needs.

Of course, eating the right foods also means *drinking* the right fluid. As you know by now, most of your body is liquid. So it is important to drink at least six glasses each day, some of it water.

This is not something that you will have to remember, though. Part of the miracle of you is that your body does the remembering for you. It reminds you when you need liquid by making you thirsty, and tells you when you need food by making you hungry.

Your Blood

IF YOU HAVE EVER held up a flashlight behind your hand, you know that it shows the inside of your fingers to be red. That is because *blood* is red, and your body has blood throughout it.

You have already read that one of the jobs of the bones is to make blood, and that the purpose of digestion is to take food to the blood. What is this wonderful substance and how does it do its many jobs?

First of all, blood is partly *fluid tissue*—which makes it different from anything else in your body. This liquid, which is more than half of your blood, is called *plasma*.

But blood also has more solid parts—*red corpuscles, platelets,* and *white corpuscles.* Most of the solid parts of blood are the red corpuscles—a quarter of a billion of them in just a single drop! They live about two months and must be replaced instantly or *anemia* will result. They are shaped like little discs curving inward to the center. These discs are red because they contain *hemoglobin,* which is a protein with iron in it.

Hemoglobin takes in *oxygen* when we breathe. Oxygen is an element from the air that all living things need. Hemoglobin then gives the oxygen to the cells that need it. When hemoglobin gets together with oxygen, it becomes a very bright red. This explains why your blood seems so much "redder" when you cut yourself than when you hold up a flashlight to your hand. The blood coming from the cut is starting to mix with the oxygen in the air.

Why does a cut always stop bleeding? The answer lies in the part of the blood called *platelets,* which are put there by nature to make the blood *clot.* Looking like

tiny plates, the platelets suddenly dissolve when they meet the oxygen in the air. What comes about is a new substance that combines with certain things in the plasma of the blood to make *fibrin*, a group of little fibers that hold back the cells of the blood like a dam holds back water.

Platelets protect us very well from outside damage, but sometimes harmful substances get into our blood through the food we eat or the air we breathe. Most sickness is caused by germs inside of us. Your *white corpuscles* fight these germs.

A white cell seems to "know" what and where germs are, and destroys them by moving to the germs and "digesting" them! Though white cells are bigger than red cells, there are far fewer of them. You have many hundreds of red corpuscles for every white one. When great numbers of germs get into the blood, your bone marrow produces more white corpuscles to battle them.

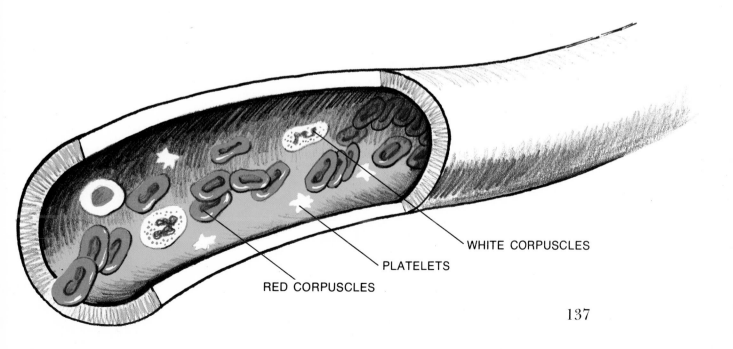

WHITE CORPUSCLES

PLATELETS

RED CORPUSCLES

White cells have no exact form, since they change their shape in order to get through the walls of the blood vessels and find the germs.

Although every person has red corpuscles, platelets, and white corpuscles, all human blood is not quite the same. People have four different types: A, B, AB, and O. Some types do not combine with others. It is important to know which blood type you have in case you ever need a *blood transfusion,* when someone else's blood is injected into you.

When you grow up, you will have about ten pints of blood in your body. This might seem like a lot until you stop to think that almost countless cells are contained in it, with eight million cells dying and being replaced every second. These new cells work tirelessly with the older ones to give your body the nourishment it needs, to repair it, and to fight sickness within it.

A Marvelous
Pumping System

IT TOOK MAN THOUSANDS of years to make a watch
that would wind itself, and even "self-winding" watches
are really wound up by the motion of your body. But
long ago nature made the *heart* so that it would beat for
a lifetime without stopping. And what your heart does
for you is more amazing than what any machine can do.

Thump — thump . . . thump — thump . . . listen to
your heart, feel its pulse in your wrist. Your heart begins
beating long before you are born and keeps up its
thump—thump year after year with the help of nerves
that direct it. Each second of each minute of each day

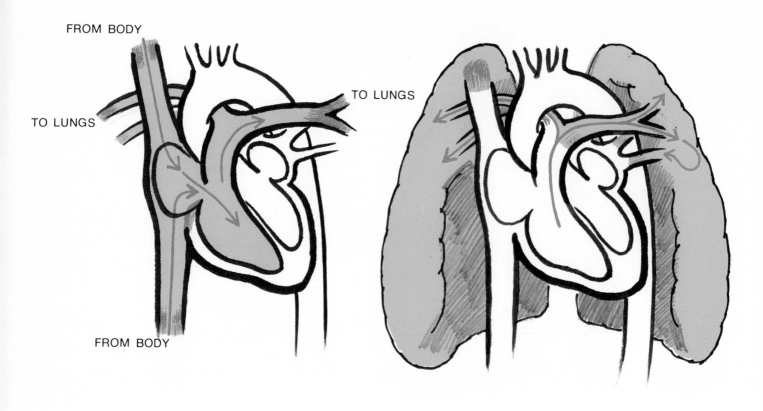

FROM BODY

TO LUNGS

TO LUNGS

FROM BODY

your heart beats inside your chest and sends blood through your whole body.

The heart is a muscle—but a different type than your other muscles—which contracts and relaxes about once a second. Each contraction-relaxation is a *heartbeat,* and pumps blood to every part of your body.

Though your heart is only about as big as your fist and doesn't even weigh a pound, it is able to beat almost a million times in a week. The trip that blood makes— from your heart to the farthest part of the body and back—takes less than sixty seconds. In seven days your heart pumps almost 100,000 quarts of blood.

The heart lies between the lungs, a little more on your left side than on your right, and is made up of four

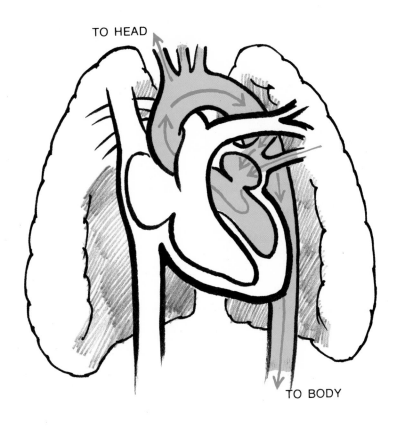

TO HEAD

TO BODY

parts or *chambers.* The upper two are called *atriums,* the lower two, *ventricles.* Each ventricle is connected to the atrium above it by a valve that sends blood down to the ventricle. From there the blood travels two main roads in its trip through your body.

When the right ventricle contracts, the blood is squeezed into a large *artery* which goes to the lungs. An artery is a tube that always takes blood away from your heart. Your blood gathers the *oxygen* it needs from the air in your lungs, and gives off the *carbon dioxide* it does not need.

The blood then flows from the lungs through two *veins*—tubes that carry blood *to* the heart—to the left atrium. From there it goes down into the left ventricle.

141

Now you have a clue as to why your heart can pump so miraculously year after year. The reason is that while part of the heart is working, the other part is resting.

When the left ventricle contracts, your blood moves into another big artery which branches off again into smaller and smaller arteries throughout your body.

The very littlest ones are in the tissues of your body themselves, and are named *capillary arteries*. They are only a single cell thick. As the blood gets to these capillary arteries, it carries the food it got from the digestive system and the oxygen it got from the lungs to the cells. It takes away waste and carbon dioxide at the same time.

As you might guess, connected to capillary arteries are *capillary veins*, which meet and form bigger and bigger veins the closer they are to the heart. You have many, many miles of capillaries in your body, though each one is smaller than any of the letters in these words you are reading. With your blood, your veins and arteries, heart and capillaries compose your body's *circulatory system*. Put them all together and they would more than go around the world!

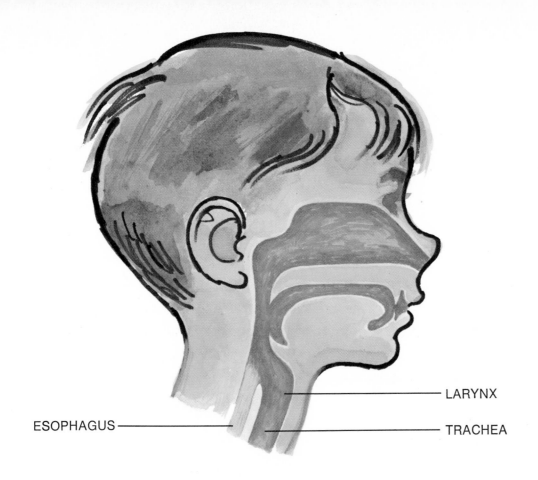

ESOPHAGUS —————————

LARYNX —————————

TRACHEA —————————

Air Is To Breathe

HOLD YOUR BREATH for as long as you can.

Hard, isn't it? The body can go for days without water and for weeks without food if it must. But your body cannot even go for a few minutes without air, because of the oxygen it contains. The more active you are, the more oxygen you will use up and so you will have to breathe faster to gain extra energy. But even when you are sleeping deeply your body needs oxygen and you must breathe several times each minute.

Breathing begins with the nostrils of the nose, though sometimes we breathe through the mouth. The

143

air goes into our throat, getting warmed if it is cold, and then down into a tube called the *trachea*.

There are many tiny hairs in the nose and mucous membranes in the throat that trap dust or germs that we might inhale. If there are too many, we cough or sneeze to get them back out. So by the time the air reaches our trachea, it is pretty pure.

The trachea turns into two parts, called *bronchial tubes*. Each one goes into a *lung*. Your two lungs are organs that grow larger when you *inhale* air, and become relaxed and smaller when you *exhale* it. Inside the lungs, the bronchial tubes branch again and again. The very smallest branches are hardly bigger than capillaries, and are named *alveoli*.

The alveoli are sacs which look like tiny balloons, and these hundreds of millions of little sacs make the lungs spongy and soft and balloon-like. These tiny bal-

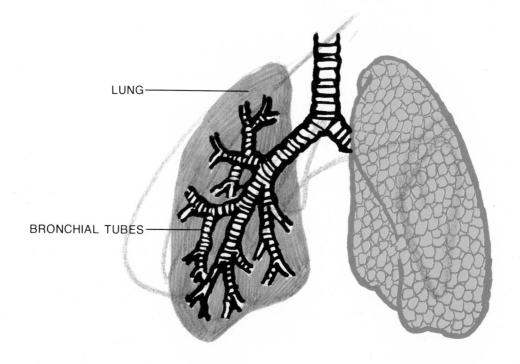

LUNG

BRONCHIAL TUBES

loons are very moist, and thus can dissolve oxygen and get it ready to enter your bloodstream. Every time you inhale, oxygen passes into your blood, and carbon dioxide moves through the walls of your veins and into the lungs to be breathed out when you exhale.

If man were not able to do these things with air, he could not live as he does. Frogs, for example, must have moisture on their skin since they breathe through it. Fish have no lungs at all, but breathe through gills and cannot survive out of the water.

When air is exhaled from your lungs, it moves up in between the pair of *vocal cords* of the *larynx* or voice box. This is how you speak. Try to talk while breathing in and you will see how important exhaling is to talking. If you are a boy, your vocal cords will become longer than a girl's when you grow up, and this will make your voice deeper.

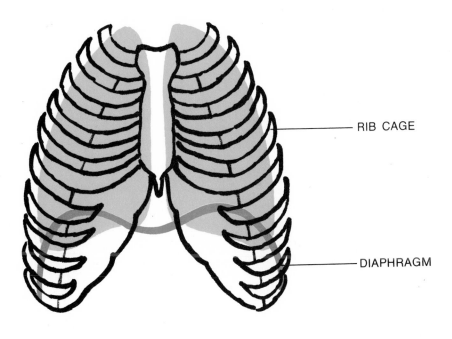

RIB CAGE

DIAPHRAGM

Below the lungs is something just as interesting as what is above them. It is a powerful, flat muscle named the *diaphragm*. When the diaphragm moves down, your ribs move up and out.

What does this do? It produces a place in the lungs in which there is not much air at all. So air immediately rushes in. When your diaphragm relaxes, your ribs move down and force the lungs to be smaller. This forces the carbon dioxide-filled air out of the lungs.

Inhaling and exhaling are also called *respiring*. All of these parts together that take in and let out air are called your *respiratory system*. You might forget to eat once in a while, but you can readily see nature has made certain that you will always "remember" to breathe.

Your Body's Covering

ONCE NATURE HAS GIVEN us muscles and bones and organs, it must give us something to cover them. This is not as simple as you might think.

You need more than a mere covering—like a cloth coat or a paper bag—to keep out dust and germs.

Your covering has to be tough, so that it can protect you from a lot more than just dust and germs. If your covering were made of paper, for example, once it got wet it would never be the same.

Your covering must be capable of repairing itself when something does happen to it. And it should be able

to do this so well that only once in a great while does it leave a patchmark or "scar."

Your covering must be flexible enough so that the muscles and bones inside can move and stretch without breaking right through it. At the same time, it mustn't be so loose as to hang down and get in your way.

Your covering must be able to feel, since touch is one of your most important senses. A cloth coat certainly cannot "sense" anything. Neither can glass or cotton or grass—or anything else except for one special something.

Your covering must not only be able to hold all-important moisture within your body, but also be capable of holding in warmth when it is cold and letting heat out on hot days.

And this is not all. Your covering must be light enough so that it does not weigh you down. And it must

be of a different thickness in different places — like very thin on your eyelids to let the morning light wake you up and very thick on the palms of your hands for hard work and play.

It is plain to see that no ordinary covering can perform all these different duties. What is really needed is an organ so special that it can spread out all over us.

The *skin* is that organ.

Even though it covers you completely from head to toe, your skin weighs only about six pounds when you are grown. If two dozen layers of it were to be placed one on top of another, they would come out to just a little more than an inch in thickness.

Yet within that "thin skin" are *melanocytes*, or cells that make your skin light or dark, as well as stopping harmful rays of the sun; sweat glands that allow you to *perspire* on warm days, as well as carrying wastes out of the body; and nerve endings and blood vessels for feeling and circulation.

Your skin is so important, in fact, that certain things about it can often tell the doctor—or even your parents—that you are sick. One of these things is when your skin becomes "flushed" from fever. At just about all other times, though, your skin holds body temperature at about 98.6 degrees, whether the temperature outside is hotter than that or below freezing.

Actually, you have two "skins." The truly sensitive one is called the *dermis.* The layer on top of the dermis is the *epidermis,* which is mostly cells that are no longer living and that wear off during our daily activities. On the outside of the epidermis are your hairs, which grow from little bulbs or *follicles* in the dermis.

Though all these many things about your skin are exactly the same as in every other person's, nature has made *your* skin different in one way. Look at the tips of your fingers and you will see little raised lines and circles. These are your *fingerprints.* No one else's are the same.

Your body's "covering" is surely far, far more amazing and useful than a cloth coat or a paper bag, isn't it?

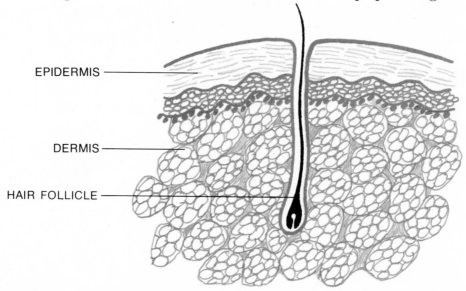

EPIDERMIS

DERMIS

HAIR FOLLICLE

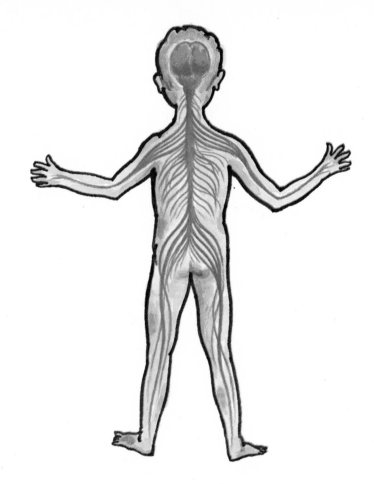

The Magic Switchboard

WHAT MAKES YOUR SENSES SENSE? Even the best camera in the world needs *someone* to take the picture.

What makes your muscles move? *You* do, could be the answer. But *who* is that "you"?

Even all the muscles of your body would not be miracles if somewhere something were not directing each one and helping them all work together. You do have just such a "director."

Think of the largest, tallest building that you can. Imagine that inside of it, on every inch of every floor, are telephones with wires running from them to other telephones. And imagine that on the top floor of this skyscraper there is a great switchboard taking all the messages from all the phones and sending them out to other phones.

Think of a dozen buildings just like this one. *That* is what it would take to make a "director" like the one you have—your *brain.*

Now think of what *you* just did.

Think of *thinking.*

Your brain not only makes miracles happen like your muscles moving or your senses sensing, but it lets you *think*—and this makes you different from any other creature on earth. It allows you not only to ride a bike, but to *decide* to ride a bike—as well as to *be able* to read a book like this one.

Without your brain, you could not only make no movements or do no thinking, but you could feel no pleasure or pain, and have no feelings like joy or surprise or even sadness.

Your brain makes your muscles and senses and everything else work through a network of nerves throughout your whole body. A *nerve* is a fiber of cells or *neurons* that is able to carry a kind of "message" along it, the way wires carry electricity. Like other cells, a neuron has a nucleus, membrane, and cytoplasm.

But a neuron also has very thin threads of protoplasm, called *dendrites,* which branch out from one side of it. On its other side, there is a thicker, fat-covered fiber called an *axon,* which can be very short or two to three feet long. Dendrites bring impulses to the cell, and axons take them away from it to a new place.

Together, axons and dendrites make a neuron different from any other cell in your body.

Nerve tissue is constructed so that the axons of one neuron "connect" to the dendrites of another. Actually, however, the two do not quite touch. The space between them is called a *synapse* and must be jumped over by an impulse that is traveling along a nerve.

Nerve cells are never replaced once they die. For this reason nature makes certain to protect them very well. One of the few places they are not well-protected is in your elbow, which is why when you hit your "funny bone," the nerves tingle up and down your whole arm.

Every one of the nerves in your body is connected to either your brain or your spinal cord. Twelve pairs of nerves go from the spinal cord into the brain. Once they get there, these nerves cross over to opposite sides. This is why the left side of your body is directed by the right side of your brain, and the right side of your body by the left side of your brain.

Another 31 pairs of nerves connect to all the organs of the body from the spinal cord. If they take impulses to the muscles, they are called *motor nerves*. If their job is to take impulses from the sense organs to the brain, they are named *sensory nerves*.

But what exactly is this all-important organ to which everything else in your body seems to respond?

Your brain is right at the top of you as a "director" should be, taking up the upper half of your skull. Its

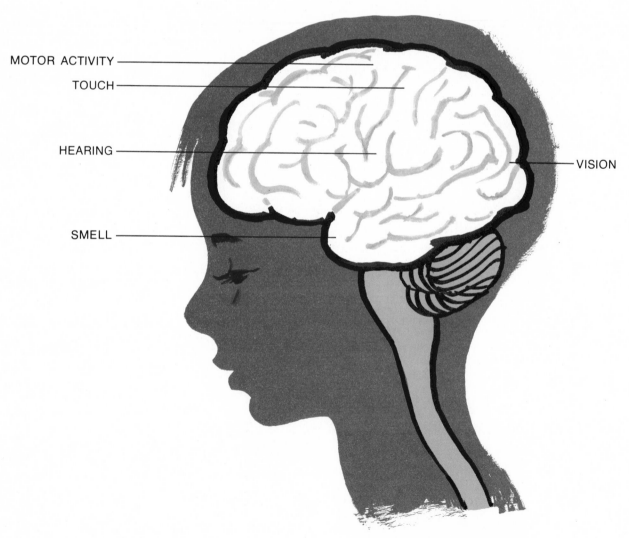

MOTOR ACTIVITY

TOUCH

HEARING

VISION

SMELL

largest part is the *cortex,* which is made up of a pair of wrinkled-looking *hemispheres* of nerves. On the outside the nerve cells are gray, which is why people sometimes call the brain "gray matter."

The most important thing about the cortex is that it is the thinking part of the brain. It lets you remember things you have done, understand things that you see, and figure out problems in school. All these are your *conscious* activities, the ones that make man able to build machines almost as amazing as his own brain.

Let us imagine, for instance, that the doorbell in your home rings. What happens is that a certain part of your cortex "hears" the sound and sends this information to another part of the cortex. In this part is your knowledge of what a ringing doorbell means. That knowledge is transferred just as instantly to still another part of the cortex, which decides to answer the doorbell. To do this, your cortex will have to send out many, many impulses so that the nerves all over your body can tell your muscles what moves to make. It may seem simple to you to answer the doorbell, but the fact is that it takes hundreds and hundreds of small actions just to move your head, walk to the door, and open it.

There are times, though—particularly when something may be harmful to you—when the brain and nerves work in a different way called a *reflex action.* Suppose you touch a very hot stove, for example. Your hand pulls away at once. This happens because the nerve impulse travels a special "shortcut." The impulse races from your skin to a sensory nerve. It reaches your spinal cord and goes immediately to a motor nerve that makes your muscles work. A reflex action like this takes less than one-tenth of a second since the impulse is traveling along its special pathway at faster than 300 feet a second. While it is rushing, your first sensory impulse is taking the usual path to your brain, and you also feel pain from the hot stove.

In the back of your skull is the part of the brain named the *cerebellum*. It also has two hemispheres which, among other things, control your sense of balance.

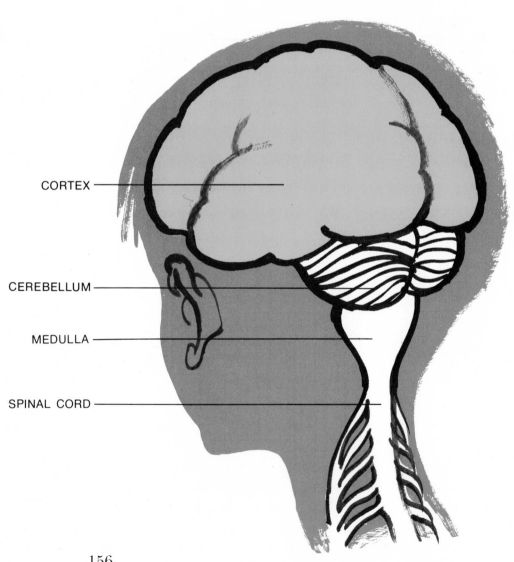

CORTEX

CEREBELLUM

MEDULLA

SPINAL CORD

Your involuntary muscles are controlled by a third part of the brain, the *medulla,* just above the spinal cord. Smaller than the cortex or the cerebellum, the medulla directs your digestion, your breathing, and the beating of your heart.

The *spinal cord* is like a cylinder, and comes down through the spinal column from the medulla. On the outside of the spinal cord are cells and blood vessels, while inside it are nerve fibers. Though this very important tissue goes most of the way down your spine, it weighs only a single ounce!

The spinal cord, the nerves that branch out from it, and the parts of your brain make up your *nervous system.* The information that they constantly supply about the "world" inside you as well as the world outside enables you to live—to do everything from moving your muscles and making things to learning and living.

Many things are still not known about this most amazing miracle of yours. And do you know what will tell us new facts about the brain? The brain itself!

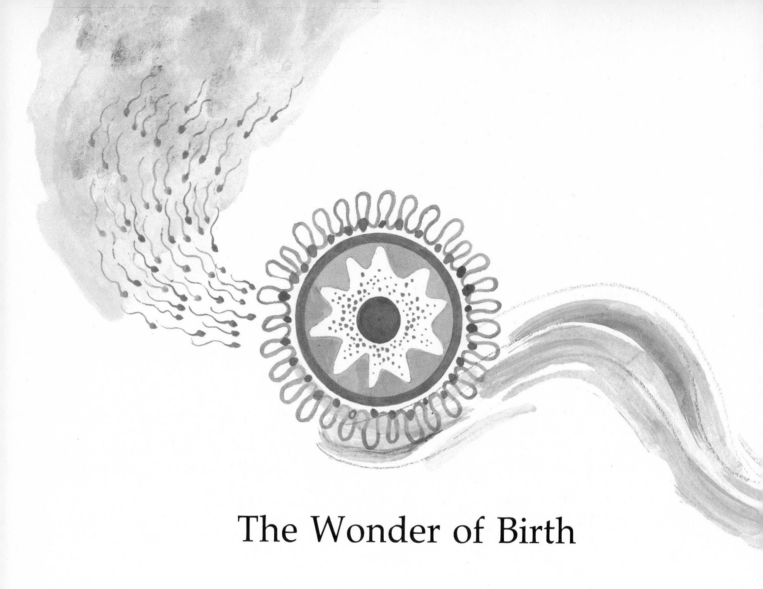

The Wonder of Birth

ANOTHER "MIRACLE" OF YOU—one as wonderful as even your heart or brain—is the way in which you first came to be alive.

The trillions and trillions of different kinds of cells that are you all come from just one cell, a special type of cell made in a special place in the body of your mother. This special cell is called an egg or *ovum*. Unlike other cells, it had only half the usual number of *chromosomes*. (These are tiny bits that make you the kind of person you are.) It became "whole" when it absorbed a *sperm* cell from your father, with another 23 chromosomes.

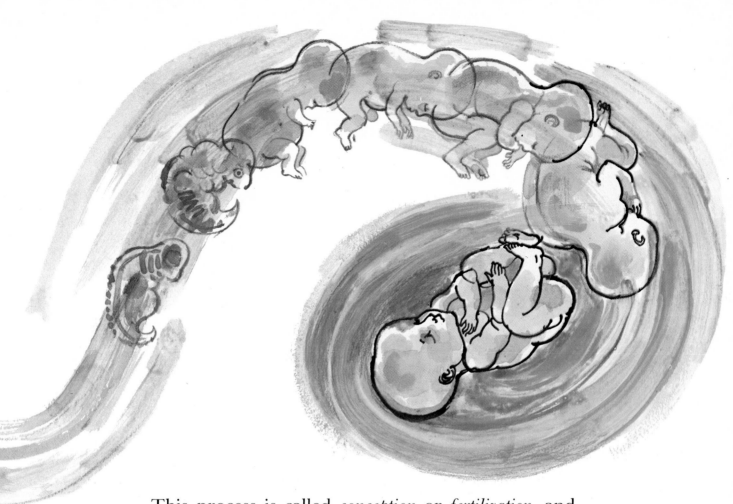

This process is called *conception* or *fertilization,* and it is the beginning of the process by which new human beings are made or *reproduced.*

For the first 24 hours after conception takes place, the new cell rests for the huge task it must perform. For during the coming months that one cell will become a complete living person!

First it grows a little bit. Next the nucleus changes, every one of the chromosomes slowly becomes two, and then the cell divides in half. Suddenly, there are two cells. Each of these grows larger and then divides again.

In a few days there are not only many more cells, but different kinds. At this point you still look pretty much like any other animal—a dog or even a frog— several days after it is conceived.

But after twelve weeks, those cells look like a human being! Before you were even two weeks old, you had a brain, and before you were a month old, your heart was beating. This is because deep inside, those cells were really like no other animal's. There were three layers of them. The outside layer was mainly to be your skin and sense organs. The middle layer would turn into your heart, bones, and muscles. The inside layer was to become your digestive system.

You probably wonder how the human *embryo* or *fetus* obtains its food when it is inside the mother's body. The answer is through an organ called the *placenta*, which sends food and oxygen through the umbilical cord attached to the embryo. When you finally come into the world, you no longer need it, so the doctor cuts off the umbilical cord. Your *navel* or "bellybutton" shows where it once was attached.

The embryo has much growing to do before it can be born from the mother's *uterus*, though. Wrapped in a sac filled with fluid, the fetus has all of its important parts when it is no longer than three inches. It stays in the uterus for nine months altogether, growing and developing as every human being does, and yet becoming an individual which will be different than any other human being. On the day that the baby is ready to be born, he comes out of the uterus to begin his life.

Your Body's Enemies

DID YOU EVER PLAY the game where a group of objects are all alike except one, and you are to choose the object that is out of place?

Now that you know the main things that belong in your body, it is important to know some of the things that do not belong inside you. Most of them are bad *bacteria* or *germs,* which are an unusual kind of one-celled being or organism. Some of them, called *viruses,* are even smaller and more unusual.

Both germs and viruses need food and certain other things in order to survive.

If somehow—through a cut or in the air you breathe or through what you eat—these bacteria or germs enter your body, they will try to find food and a home in it. The other cells in your body must fight and destroy them if you are to stay alive and healthy.

Germs or viruses are what make you have a cold or cough. The moment that they invade your body, it begins battling them, and usually within a day or two your sneezing, coughing and fever are gone.

The same thing is true of *chicken pox,* a disease which you will probably catch while you are young—if you have not already had it. This is because chicken pox is very easily transmitted from one person to another—that is, it is easy to "catch." With this sickness, you have fever and a rash over some parts of your body. With rest, however, your body will be back to normal in a few days.

Mumps is also very catching and a bit more serious. The glands in the neck swell and it hurts to talk or eat. After a week or so, though, good care will cure the

mumps. And, like chicken pox, once you get the mumps, you cannot catch it again. You are what is called "immune." There are other germ diseases, though, that are far more dangerous.

One of these diseases is *smallpox*. It has many painful symptoms, one of which is severe sores over the entire body. Even when the body wins its battle over smallpox, there may be many ugly scars where these sores were.

Tetanus or lockjaw is an even more harmful sickness, in which a person cannot open his mouth and has much trouble breathing. Very few people with tetanus ever get better, and so, just as with smallpox, the best way to deal with it is to *prevent* it. This is why the doctor gives you *vaccinations* and other shots that protect you against such enemies. Nearly all children get shots for these two diseases, and for other sicknesses like *polio, diphtheria,* and even *measles*. Shots may not be much fun, but now these diseases, which used to kill thousands of people every year, hurt almost no one.

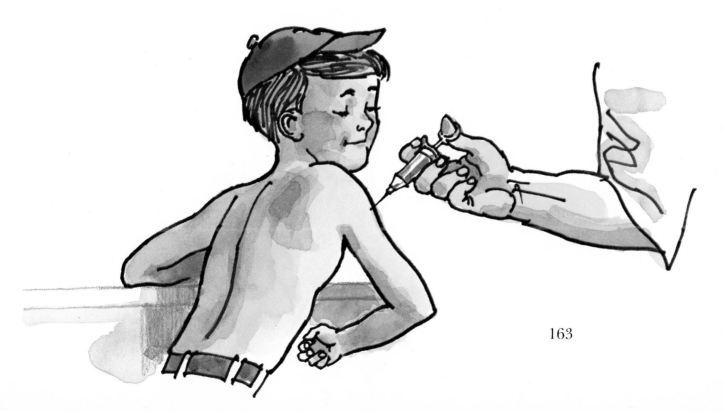

Keeping Fit

"MAKE A MUSCLE."

No doubt you have said that to your father—or heard him say it to you—many times. The biceps muscle of your upper arm is the "muscle" you are referring to, but you *really* mean the "extra" muscle there that you have gotten from working or playing hard.

For just as the lungs nature gave you are used and made better through breathing, so the many muscles of your body grow stronger and larger when you use them. You must exercise your muscles every day. And as your muscles are used in exercise, your heart and lungs and every other part of your body become much stronger and healthier.

Exercise makes the heart pump faster and push more blood into the tissues. In this way every part of your body is given nourishment and cleaned out as well. Exercise also makes you breathe deeper, and thus gets rid of the carbon dioxide deep in your lungs. And exercise builds up your muscles by forcing the cells to grow larger to do the task before them. A muscle is only as strong as you make it by using it often. So your body's biggest enemy of all—bigger than any germ—can be *not* using your muscles enough.

If you are in good health to start with, it is almost impossible to use your muscles *too much,* because they will "tell" you when they are too tired to do any more. And as far as your heart is concerned, it is the *last* thing that will tire. It can do as much work each day as it would take to lift twenty-five tons!

In recent years, there has been much talk about which is the best of what seem like many, many kinds of exercise. The truth is that there are three main types of exercise. Though each helps your body in every way, one kind of exercise is best for *flexibility* and *coordination,* another kind for *endurance* and *health,* and a third kind of exercise for *strength.*

CALISTHENICS

Calisthenics, the first basic kind of exercise, stretch your muscles and teach them to work together. By doing calisthenics for just five minutes a day, you can soon move more gracefully and take part better in different sports and games.

Here is a beginning calisthenics program, which can be done in your own room every morning.

Bend down and touch your toes with your hands without bending your knees. Do this five times the first week and then start adding one more each new week until you reach twenty-five. If you cannot get all the way down, just go as far as you can go. By going a little farther each day, you will soon be reaching your toes. Within a few months you may even be able to touch the floor with the palms of your hands.

Next, "shake hands" above your head. Then, with your hands held together, move them in a big wide circle in front of you, from right to left five times, then from left to right five times.

CALISTHENICS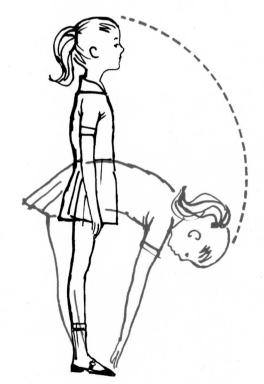

Finally, standing with your feet together and your hands at your sides, spread your feet apart to the sides with a jump while you swing your arms upward and clap your hands above your head. Then, without stopping, bring your arms back down to your sides and your feet back together. Repeat this until you have done it twenty-five times.

INTERVAL

The second kind of exercise, though, takes longer than calisthenics. Called "interval" exercise, it was discovered by the President's Council on Physical Fitness, and always needs thirty minutes to do. It is worth the time, however, because this type of exercise is what makes your heart and lungs stronger, and turns the

deep fat in your tissues to healthier things. This will allow you to work and play longer without getting tired.

Doctors and athletic teachers have found that the body needs to exercise for half an hour *without stopping* to do these things. But no one can exercise very hard for thirty minutes without some kind of rest. So interval training gives you periods of *lesser exercise* when your body does not have to work so hard, but the good processes started by the exercise still go on in your body.

These same doctors and athletic teachers have also found that running is by far the best interval exercise. But to get the full benefits of running, you must know *how* to run. And to learn how to run, you must first learn how to walk.

Practice walking with your arms swinging freely at your sides. When you move, "spring" a little, and use the front part of your feet. Your chest should always be out and your stomach in.

INTERVAL

*to learn how to run
you must first learn
how to walk . . .*

Once you learn to walk like this, you will do a lot better at running. Your toes will be pointing straight ahead, and the movement of one leg will seem to make the next one happen almost as if your body were a well-oiled machine. It will seem almost as if you couldn't stop if you wanted to.

One foot and then the other will swing forward. When your back foot is lifted, it will kick high. Your body will lean slightly forward. Your arms will swing in rhythm with your legs, your hands swinging up above your waist.

Now, run as fast as you can for one minute. Then walk for a while. When you feel more rested, begin your running again, only this time not as fast. After you become tired, walk once more. Keep this up—running with intervals of walking—for thirty minutes. After a few weeks, you will find that you are running faster and for more of the time.

ISOMETRICS

The third kind of exercise is called *isometric* and *isotonic,* and builds power in your muscles. There are many kinds of exercises that you can do to increase your strength. One of the best is "push-ups." To do push-ups, lie face down on the floor, and push your whole body up with just your hands. The body must be kept straight while you are pushing, however. Start by doing as many push-ups as you can, and then add one more each week. Soon you will really be able to "make a muscle," since this exercise is one that helps develop the biceps. Clasping your hands tightly together and pulling them as hard as you can is another exercise that makes your muscles stronger.

Before developing the muscles in your arms and legs, though, it is important to build the muscles in the

ISOMETRICS

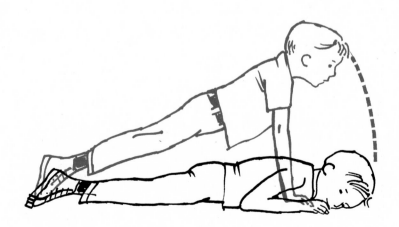

middle of you. Good "stomach muscles" will keep your back straight and your chest out. And the two best exercises for a strong middle are "leg-raises" and "sit-ups."

To do a leg-raise, lie flat on your back with your feet together. Without bending your legs, lift them until they are almost straight up. Then slowly let them down to the floor and begin again.

A sit-up starts much the same way. To do a sit-up, lie flat on your back with your hands clasped behind your head, your knees bent, and your feet flat on the floor. Sit up and touch your kneecaps with your elbows. Then lie back down and do it again. Start with five leg-raises and five sit-ups, and add one more of each exercise every week.

Many young people have the idea that exercising is not nearly as much fun as playing games. But the truth is that you can make a "game" out of exercising.

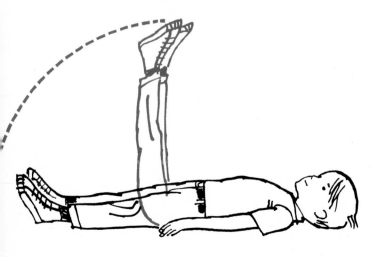
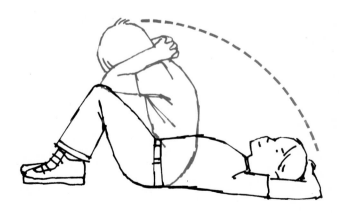

How? By trying to do just a little bit better each time. And by realizing that you are playing against the hardest opponent of all—yourself.

Of course, games with others are still a great deal of fun. Games like basketball, baseball, volleyball, and field hockey are very fine for *keeping* you in shape once your program of more basic exercises *gets* you in shape.

Exercise and games give you even more than good health. You will have more energy and feel better, and you will know that you are winning the battle over your body's greatest enemy. For just as your brain is a great gift which must be used to make it work, so your body's muscles and inner systems must be used to their fullest so that you can be truly healthy.

Health Rules

HAVE YOU EVER SEEN someone who had trained his mind to remember a great number of things? Well your body can be trained just as your mind can.

What should you teach it?

To keep the body nature gave you in a healthy condition, there is much more to do than exercise.

For example, you must *breathe*. But we all do that, you may answer. If we didn't breathe, we couldn't live. Yet do you breathe the *right way*? Most people do not. If you learn to breathe correctly early in life, it will help your health for the rest of your life.

Good breathing should be deep and slow and easy. You should really try to enjoy the air you take into your lungs, just as you enjoy the food that you put into your mouth.

At first you may find deep breathing a difficult habit to form. The best way to overcome this is to practice taking in a deep breath and holding it while you count ten to yourself. Once a day you might also try to hold your breath for as long as you can. This helps to exercise the capacity of your lungs, which means that more oxygen can be supplied to your cells.

The *food* you give your body is also important. A special kind of "food" that you take into your system is water. Even though it does not actually nourish you, water makes up most of your tissues. You should drink several glasses of water a day.

Your body will tell you when you are hungry. Usually, three good meals a day and a snack of fresh fruits or raw vegetables before bedtime are enough to satisfy your hunger. If you do not have a good appetite at meals, it is probably because you are eating between meals or not getting enough exercise.

Overeating and lack of exercise can cause you to gain more weight than you should. Extra weight is a burden on your heart and other tissues. There is no really good weight chart for young people, since they grow at different rates and have different bone structures. But if you can pinch your waist and find more than an inch of skin, you may be getting fat.

Sleep is another important health need of your body. You usually need ten hours, and possibly a nap or short

rest period at some other time during the day. Keep one window open for fresh air when you sleep.

The reason you must rest is that being tired or feeling *fatigue* is simply a result of too many wastes building up inside you. As your muscles are constantly moved throughout the day, they create more waste material than your body can get rid of. Rest gives your system time to get rid of wastes, and to build up energy for the next day of activity. And there is no better kind of rest than sleep. Training your body to go to sleep and to wake up at a certain time of each night and day is one of the finest health rules.

The way you "carry" your body — its *posture* — is important, because good posture puts your lungs in the right place so you can inhale the way you should. Proper posture is also good for your back and leg muscles, and helps the organs of your abdomen function better.

Sunlight is a healthy thing for your body, since it produces Vitamin D inside you, kills germs on your skin, and is good for your blood. At the same time, you must be careful not to get too much sun, or to open your eyes too wide for a long time when the sun is very bright.

A final "health" rule is to make time during each day to do things that are hard for you, whether it be your schoolwork or learning a new skill, and also to make time to have fun! The work and play that you do should be balanced, just as everything inside you is balanced by nature.

Remember, health is much more than not being sick. Health is a good, energetic, positive feeling that you have throughout your whole body and mind.

Good Grooming

EXERCISE AND RULES of health are things that will help you keep the *inside* of you as it should be. But the *outside* is also important. Keeping it clean and neat is called *grooming*.

The most obvious part outside you is your skin, of course, and the best way to keep it clean is by taking a bath or a shower every day. Your pores give off waste material which should be washed away. This is true especially in summer, when you perspire almost all the time if you are outside. You might even need more than one bath or shower a day.

Your hands, however, always need to be washed more than once a day. Almost every time you touch something with them, there is a chance that bacteria will be transferred to you. You should always wash your hands before meals.

Keeping your face clean is as important as washing your hands. This is the part of your body which others see first. It is also the part which gets blemishes the most easily when it is not kept clean. Make it a rule to wash your face whenever you wash your hands—and whenever you want to look your best.

Your hair is a very important part of the outside of you. If you treat it right, it will crown you with a shiny, healthy look. The best way to do this is by brushing—

one hundred strokes each day whether you are a girl or a boy. Brushing not only takes out loose hair, it cleans away dandruff and dirt.

After you brush your hair, it helps to put your fingers at the back of your head and move them firmly toward the front a number of times. The natural oils of the skin on your head or your *scalp* are mostly in the back, and it is best to move some to the front. After you have done this a few times, take a look at your hands and you will actually see the oil.

Naturally, your hair should look combed and neat as much as possible. It is simple to carry a comb with you during the day and run it through a few times after your hair has gotten out of place. In the morning you

will be able to take your time fixing your hair in front of a mirror. There will be times when your hair is very dry. If so, you may want to use a hair tonic with *lanolin,* which is a fatty substance often obtained from sheep.

Once every few days (more often for girls than for boys) you will also need to shampoo your hair with a mild soap. And once every few weeks (much less often for girls than for boys) you will need a haircut.

Another part of good grooming is your teeth. There are few things as attractive as a nice smile. You surely know that it is important to brush after meals. The reason for this is that your mouth is a breeding place for bacteria, which can give off something that dissolves the enamel of the teeth. Sugar also hurts them, and

little pieces of bread and certain other foods can become caught between your teeth, turn to sugar because of the digestive juices in your mouth, and give you decayed holes or *cavities* in them.

Keeping your nails, on feet as well as hands, trimmed and clean is also a part of your grooming. So are shined shoes, clean underwear, and neat clothes.

Also important is good posture—head held high in the air, shoulders straight but relaxed, chest out, stomach flat. If you don't think that posture is a part of grooming, as well as health, ask yourself how many times you have been able to tell who someone far away was before you could see his face. This is because the way that a person carries himself is part of the way he looks.

Safety Rules

BEFORE YOU EVER READ THIS book, you knew what a wonderful and exciting place this world is to live in. Now you know what a wonderful and exciting place your body is—and how to keep it that way.

You have discovered that part of what makes your body exciting is its muscles, and how it breathes, and that it can think. And you also have learned that your muscles and lungs and brain must be used properly in order to perform their daily "miracles."

In much the same way, you must know how to use the man-made "miracles" of the world around you. If you do, they will be even more exciting and wonderful. But if you don't, you may have an accident.

SAFETY AT HOME

Many "miracles" of the world are right in your own house. Most people think of home as the safest place in the world, but the fact is that more people hurt themselves at home than at any other place.

Have you ever thought about *stairs,* for example? If we didn't have them, we would have to *climb* up to the second or third floor—or maybe never even be able to go there at all. Stairs are useful, but they can be dangerous, too. Do not run up or down stairs because there is a danger of falling. Remember not to leave things on stairs, because other people might not see them, and trip or fall.

Floors are wonderful, too. They keep all the bugs and dampness and germs from the ground out of our homes. But slippery floors are not safe to run on.

Electricity is surely a "miracle" of the world around us. But you must never experiment with it until you are grown and understand it fully. Lamps make our houses bright in the night, but they can be very dangerous if you touch their cords or wires, especially if your shoes are damp. The outlets in the wall are also very dangerous.

Another wonderful thing is the stove. But unless you are big enough to help your mother in the kitchen, you should not go near the stove when something is cooking on it, because a pot or pan—as well as the hot food in it—can burn you.

There is also a place in your house, though, that you should stay even farther away from than you do from the stove. This is the medicine cabinet. As you know, medicines can sometimes help you to get well when you are sick. But they can also do the opposite—they can make you sick when you are well. Make it a firm rule that you will never put anything in your mouth except food and, if you are sick, only the medicine your parents give you.

If you forget this rule, you might choke on what doesn't belong in your mouth or, if you swallow something that isn't food, it may turn out to be poisonous.

There are poisons around every house, however, which don't even need to be swallowed to get into your body. Many things that your mother uses in cleaning, or your father keeps in the garage or basement, can hurt you even if you just drop some on your skin or breathe their fumes. That's why, if you are not familiar with what is in a certain container, it is a wise idea never to get too close to it—especially if you are not outdoors.

You should always be careful with any tools or toys you use. If you ever see a real gun, tell an adult right away—but do not bring it to him. A gun is most dangerous, and no child should touch one. And be especially watchful when you are around sharp or pointed objects. If you are carrying scissors, point them down as you walk. Of course, you know never to run with anything sharp, even a pencil or a stick.

If you see a pin or a tack on the floor, pick it up. And if you ever break something made of glass, be sure every bit of it is cleaned away.

Sometimes, though, it is hard to get up every little piece of glass. That's why it is a good idea to always wear shoes or houseslippers when you are walking around inside your home.

Once in a while, you will get cut by something sharp. When this happens, wash the cut carefully and have someone put some medicine on it. If it is a very deep cut, be sure to tell an adult, because you might need to have the doctor look at it.

SAFETY OUTDOORS

Safety is just as important when you leave your home to go other places. Sometimes you will get from one place to another by taking a car or bus. One very important rule is never to get on or off a car or bus while it is moving. If you are waiting for a car or bus to pick you up, wait on the curb or in a safety zone.

If you are walking, be careful always to stay on the sidewalk. Sometimes, though, you may be in a place where there is no sidewalk and where the only place to walk on is the road. In that case, walk on the left side of the road so you can see the cars coming toward you. Stay as far off the road as possible.

186

Always do what the traffic signals tell you, of course. Red means *stop*. Yellow means *wait*. Green means *go*. Never cross in the middle of the street. And always stop when you pass a driveway, just as you would at a busy street corner.

Sometimes you may even go somewhere on a bicycle. When you do, even if it is only a short way, remember to follow the same rules that apply to automobiles. Always make sure that your bell or horn is working, so that you can let someone in a car, who might not see you, know that you are there. When you bicycle with friends, always ride one behind the other. Try not to stop quickly unless you really have to, and never, never fool around when you are riding a bike.

SAFETY AT SCHOOL

The most important place that a bus or car, a bike or your feet will take you is to *school*. There you should follow the same rules that you do at home, plus some new ones.

One of the things we all take for granted is the chair we sit in. But because you have to sit in a chair for long periods without getting up, now and then you may want to tip back your chair. This is a very dangerous thing to do because you could easily fall over backwards.

Another thing that can bring harm to you is hurrying in the corridors. Follow the same rules there that you would while walking in traffic, for people can bump into you and hurt you just as a car can. If you are working in the school shop, wear what you are given to guard your body and eyes.

One of the things you will do for fun in school is to play games and take part in athletics. There are rules for each game that you play, and, if you follow these rules, you should not get hurt.

SAFETY IN SPORTS

Swimming is a lot of fun, but is also full of risks. A swimming pool or a lake is many times more danger-ous than a bathtub, because it is many times larger. The first and most important safety rule to follow while swimming is—*learn to swim*. Even though you are not a fish who lives in water, you will find that swimming is not hard at all. But even after you have learned to swim, there are some very important rules that you must observe for your own safety.

Never swim alone. And make sure that one of the people you are with has taken a life-saving course. Next, unless you are an expert swimmer, do not go in water that is above your neck. Also, never go into the water for forty-five minutes after you have eaten. And, of course, keep away from diving boards in pools and from boats in lakes or rivers. If a storm seems to be coming up, leave the water immediately.

In the winter you may skate on the same water in which you used to swim. But that does not mean that it is safe. Never skate or even walk on ice that has not been tested carefully and approved as safe.

When you plan to take a hike, make sure to dress properly, and especially to wear the proper type of shoes. If you are too far from home when bad weather comes up, find shelter as soon as you can. If you happen to be out in an open area and there is lightning in the sky, lie flat until you can get inside, and stay away from trees.

Above all, do not go near wild animals even if they look friendly. You should not even pet dogs and cats you do not know, since they may have a disease which you can catch.

It may seem to you that there are a lot of rules to remember in order to be safe. But once you learn them, they will become habits. Then, you can enjoy all the thrilling things in the world without putting yourself in any danger at all.